P9-DWY-034

INTERNATIONAL RELATIONS
IN POLITICAL THEORY

Related Titles from Open University Press

INTERNATIONAL RELATIONS IN POLITICAL THEORY

Howard Williams

Open University Press
Milton Keynes • *Philadelphia*

YEARY LIBRARY
LAREDO JUNIOR COLLEGE
LAREDO, TEXAS

YEARY LIBRARY
LAREDO COMM. COLLEGE
LAREDO, TEXAS

Open University Press
Celtic Court
22 Ballmoor
Buckingham
MK18 1XW

and

1900 Frost Road, Suite 101
Bristol, PA 19007, USA

First Published 1992

Copyright © Howard Williams 1992

All rights reserved. No part of this publication may be
reproduced, stored in a retrieval system or transmitted in
any form or by any means, without written permission from the
publisher.

British Library Cataloguing-in-Publication Data

Williams, Howard
  International relations in political theory.
  I. Title
  327.101

  ISBN 0-335-15628-2
  ISBN 0-335-15627-4 pbk

Library of Congress Cataloguing-in-Publication Data number available

JX
1391
.W56
1992   FEB 0 7 1994

Typeset by Gilbert Composing Services, Leighton Buzzard
Printed in Great Britain by Biddles Limited, Guildford and Kings Lynn

For Ceri

CONTENTS

PREFACE AND ACKNOWLEDGEMENTS

This book examines international relations as a theme in political theory. It is doubly introductory. First, it introduces political theory, and second, it introduces some representative problems in the study of international politics. The intended readership is first- and second-year undergraduates in politics and international relations. It would be gratifying to think that the book was also accessible to the interested layperson and possibly the practising politician. The book presupposes no great command of either political theory or international relations but does presume an interest in the issues raised.

The selection of writers looked at is personal if not wholly arbitrary. These writers represent, in my opinion, some of the more significant and interesting political theorists. If there is a bias it is perhaps towards the philosophically more weighty theorists. This is because I find such thinkers challenging and interesting, and believe that they have a great deal to say about the issues of world politics.

In a sense the fact that many of these thinkers, such as Aristotle and Hobbes, address international relations seemingly only indirectly, is the challenge. Many of the thinkers I have neglected to deal with have possibly given more attention to international relations but they are not, I believe, such significant theorists. Inevitably I will be deemed to have left out important figures both in the history of political thought and in the history of international relations thought. But I am prepared to brave the storms of such criticism in order to make a start on what I see as an important subject.

There is another selective aspect to my approach. I have concentrated on only a narrow range of topics in the political theory of each figure. Some limitation is necessary in an introductory work of this kind, but I have tried to base my selection on two considerations. First, I have tried to concentrate on what I regard as the central themes of the political theorist concerned. Second, I have tried to deal with those aspects of the theorist's ideas which bear most relevance to international relations. The reader has to judge the degree of success I have attained in pursuing these two aims.

I quite naturally come to the conclusion that the study of classical political theory is valuable for the understanding of international relations. In some respects I have also come to the more interesting conclusion that the study of political theory *is* the study of international relations. This book is about justice, the state, the conduct of politics, the understanding of international relations, war and the pursuit of peace. These are all topics for political theory which are also topics for international relations.

This is a book about political theory from the international perspective; if one wishes, it is a book about international political theory. I take it that international political theory has to do with the conduct of relations among states. I think that there are two significant senses in which international political theory has to do with the conduct of relations among states. In the first sense international political theory may try to offer an explanation or, more modestly, an interpretation of the nature of those relations. Here the emphasis is on detached observation and disinterested enquiry. In a second sense international political theory may also try to offer some suggestions about the practice of international relations. Writers on international political theory may also want to alter world society in one way or another.

I see both these activities as legitimate aspects of international political theory. In very many instances, it is very difficult to separate thinkers' understanding of international society from the practices they would like to see adopted. Classical political theory provides a rich source of knowledge in both these dimensions.

My thanks to Tony Evans and Ken Booth for helping me focus on the problems of international politics. My thanks also to Susan Shell, Ernest Fortin and Steven Smith for their kind hospitality on a recent visit to the United States. Jennifer, Wyn and Huw also deserve a mention since they are a constant reminder of the continuity between relations among individuals and relations among states.

1 PLATO: JUSTICE AND THE RULE OF PHILOSOPHERS

Plato was born in Athens in the year 427 BC when the civilization of ancient Greece was at its height. He belonged to an old and distinguished aristocratic family with many political connections.

Had it not been for one great event in his life Plato himself would probably have chosen a political career. That event was the death of the philosopher Socrates. In the year 399 BC Socrates was put on trial by the citizens of Athens charged with corrupting youth with his instruction.[1] Socrates' great teaching was that no knowledge was certain. He himself professed to be ignorant. He was never a popular philosopher for the very reason that his tireless questioning and examination of the views of others undermined their beliefs. Socrates was not an enemy of knowledge, rather he was an enemy of dogmatism.

Plato felt that the charges brought against him were entirely unjust. The sentence of death passed on Socrates disillusioned him entirely. He turned his back on practical politics and devoted himself to philosophy. Sometime during the years 388–369 BC Plato took the important step of founding the Academy. This was an establishment of learning: in many respects this school was the parent of all subsequent universities. The Academy was founded as a school for statesmen. Plato no doubt saw it as an opportunity to right some of the wrongs he saw taking place around him in Athenian society. This is where his masterpiece *The Republic* originated.

One of the famous claims of *The Republic* is that the world will know no rest or security until philosophers are statesmen. Plato always hoped to prove the truth of this claim. And it was with this purpose in mind that he travelled to Syracuse (Sicily) in 367 BC. He was invited by one of the King's advisers to come and train Dionysius II as a philosopher-ruler. It need hardly be said that the visit was not a success. Dionysius did not turn out to be a good pupil. But it would be wrong to think Plato's ideas were without their practical impact because there were other small kingdoms in the Greek World which sought with some success to implement his aims. And one of Plato's pupils, Aristotle, was also to become the tutor of Alexander the Great.

The Republic

At one point in this work Plato asks us to imagine the condition of men living in a huge underground chamber. There is only one source of light, with a long, straight passage leading towards it. In this cavern men have lived from childhood chained by their legs and their necks. They cannot move and, in consequence, they can see only directly ahead of themselves. A fire is lit and is burning brightly behind them some distance higher up in the cave. Men are working on a road at this higher level, but they are not directly visible because there is a wall between them and the cavern. The only thing which the men who are chained to the floor of the cavern can see of them is their reflections cast by the fire on the wall of the cave. They see the shadows of these men and hear the echoes of their voices from the sides of the cave.

This would be a strange and weird world. But Plato thinks that this is something like the position of the ordinary person in real life. The men chained at the bottom of the cave would take the shadows to be the real individuals; they would take the echoes to be the true voices of those individuals. Chained as they were there is little else the men could do other than to take the appearances and the sounds as the real world.

Plato presents a view of political theory which has been extremely influential throughout the ages. He conceives of the political philosopher as being in the role of a prisoner freed from the dark rigours of life in the cave. The concerns of the ordinary person, he implies, make it exceedingly difficult for him to know what is true about the world. Ordinary life is a confusion of conflicting events *which gives rise to an infinite variety of views and opinions – all claiming to be true.* Political philosophy for Plato must look beyond these disputes of ordinary everyday life to discover what is of lasting consequence.

The method of Plato's major work in political theory, *The Republic*, is to seek to raise the individual's comprehension above that of the prejudice and opinions of everyday discourse. And no one can doubt that in politics and international relations the varieties of opinion are immense. Plato employs a method called *dialectic* which he derived from the work of Socrates. He acknowledges this indebtedness by naming his principal character in *The Republic*'s dialogues Socrates. Despite its impressive sounding name *dialectic* as Plato employs it is really quite straightforward. What Plato tries to do is to draw his philosophical conclusions from the arguments currently held by public opinion in the Athens of his day. Various individuals are allowed to represent these views and they are refined and then criticized by Socrates in the dialogues.

Plato proceeds to his own vision of justice indirectly. There are three ordinary ideas of justice that he wishes to criticize and in the process of doing so he paves the way for his own conception. Those three ideas are

1 that Justice is honesty in word and deed
2 that Justice is helping friends and harming enemies
3 that Justice is always the interest of the stronger party.[2]

All three views of justice seem at first sight to be highly plausible. The first idea that we should always tell the truth and pay back anything we have received from others seems most persuasive. But Socrates argues that it is not always right or just to give people back something which is theirs. For example, it might not be right to return something to another if they intended causing harm with it. It would seem both unjust and imprudent to return a weapon to a friend who had just taken leave of his senses. We might also not want to return a car to an acquaintance if she was obviously drunk and incapable of driving it. And in the international sphere we might not want to return a colony to its original parent state where that parent state is under the rule of a cruel dictator. Justice is more general – or universal – than merely returning debts and not telling lies.

The view that justice is helping friends and harming our enemies is, in Plato's view, similarly flawed. One difficulty which immediately occurs with this view is how do we establish who is our friend and who is our enemy. People of *bad judgement* will always be harming their friends and helping their enemies when they are seeking to apply justice. Similarly, politicians of bad judgement might well ally with the least dependable states. A second problem which Plato raises is how can it possibly be just to do anyone harm? Ordinary social norms might condone such behaviour towards someone who has harmed our interests, especially if this involved exacting a legal punishment, but it can hardly present our universal standard of justice. Harming individuals affects their capacity to act justly, just as harming Germany after the First World War led to a desire for revenge. A badly treated individual or state will not behave morally. If acting justly were to harm our enemies, justice would have been employed to bring about precisely the opposite. Justice would be being unjust to others.

Plato faces his most difficult task in dealing with the third definition of justice. It is probably true that most laws are enacted by the ruling group in a state and for the most part reflect their interests. There seems then a bias in all existing justice towards the powers that be. For instance, it might be argued that existing international law reflects most adequately the interests of the developed industrial states and tends to overlook the claims of the

Third World. If this is so it might seem that Third World states may have less reason to abide by international law than developed states. But if international law begins only to count partially as a result of such perceptions then it may not be taken to embody justice in any attractive sense.

Plato suggests that this realist view of justice shares the same difficulty as the previous two. It is a view of justice which applies to one particular way of acting – here acting in the interests of the stronger party. But this practice can be carried out well or badly. The stronger party may misconceive its own interest and enact laws which work against it. Then existing justice would not be the interest of the stronger party, it would be the interest of the subordinate groups.

Furthermore, Plato does not accept that the interests of the ruling group are always opposed to those of the people subordinate to them. If we take ruling to be a skill like that of the doctor then the aim of ruling cannot be merely to pursue one's own interest. As a ruler, individuals best serve their own interest by ruling well. They cannot rule well without considering the interests of those people they are governing. Thus, ruling can just as much be seen as serving the interests of the subordinate group as manipulating them. *The ship's captain does not exercise authority over his crew merely for his own sake, but for their sake as well.*[3] There is no reason why in serving our own interests we might not also be serving the interests of others. And it is on the basis of such a notion of interdependence that Plato develops his own view of justice.

Justice in the individual and the state

Communities come into being in the first place because individuals are not self-sufficient. Our first and greatest need is, of course, the provision of food to keep us alive, our second need is shelter, our third, clothing of various kinds. To supply these needs we require other people. We need farmers to produce the food, weavers to produce clothing, shoemakers to produce shoes, and so on. So even supplying the simplest human needs breeds interdependence. Plato goes on to outline in more detail all the individuals and skills that are required to provide for the more complex human needs, giving rise naturally to commerce and industry. Various groups then come into being in society carrying out the various types of work. Moreover a healthy state does *not merely provide for our physical needs:* within it there are 'a multitude of occupations none of which is concerned with necessities'. A healthy society requires as well as farmers and business people, 'artists, sculptors, painters and musicians'.[4] For its defence and its well-being it will also require armed forces: an army and a navy. So from the primitive society where only our most basic needs are catered for Plato leads us on to a sophisticated society which relies on an advanced division of labour to supply its wants.

What does justice consist of in such a mature society? When Plato is discussing the development of society he claims that *society develops most rapidly where each person sticks to his own skill. This view is that 'one man could not do more than one job or profession well'.*[5] Individuals have a task for which they are more naturally suited. Some people have a talent for writing, others have the ability to shape things with their hands. It goes without saying that the first should be authors, and the second should become craftworkers. This gives us a natural division of labour to which we should keep. And this is what justice is in the state for Plato. It is minding one's business, or 'keeping to what belongs to one and doing one's own job'.[6] Interference of the classes of a society with each other's jobs 'does the greatest harm to our state, and we are entirely justified in calling it the worst of all evils'.[7] Justice is to be found in the society which is rigidly divided into classes according to ability. This specialization also runs into the military sphere. Plato thinks it vitally important that the business of war should be run by those who are most competent in that sphere and he would have a special group, whom he calls the auxiliaries, to prosecute the task.

Plato deals with justice in the individual in a way which is analogous with his treatment of justice in society. Here also all rests upon a proper division of labour. Plato suggests there are three aspects or parts to the human soul. First, there is *reason*, the faculty which calculates and divides. Second, there is *desire*, or appetite which derives from our merely instinctive and physical needs. Third, there is an aspect of the soul which lies midway between reason and desire. We might call this *passion*. Reason is the *reflective element* in the mind; and the element which feels hunger and thirst 'and the agitations of sex and other desires' is the irrational appetite. Our third aspect can be subject to either our irrational appetite or our reason. But passion is never purely rational nor is it purely instinctive. Nowadays, we might refer to this third aspect of the soul as our emotions.

By analogy with justice in the state each of these three parts of the soul should take its proper place in relation to the others.

> The just man will not allow the three elements which made up his inward self to trespass on each other's functions or interfere with each other, but, by keeping all three in tune, like the notes of a scale (high, middle and low or whatever they be), will in the truest sense set his house in order, and be his own lord and master and be at peace with himself.[8]

When the passions and appetite are under the control of reason the individual has the potential to be just. Where there is a dispute among the three elements of the soul and one is not properly subordinate to the other, confusion, injustice, indiscipline and cowardice all follow. The statesman must exercise this kind of self-control.

In the discussion with Thrasymachus in *The Republic* Plato takes to task those who question the utility of justice. He raises here a very knotty problem of personal morality and social responsibility. Does it pay to be just? This problem arises in a particularly acute way in international society where there is a dispute not only about the nature of justice but also about who is to enforce it.

Plato believes the answer to this must be yes. No society – not even a society of thieves – would be possible if everyone were systematically unjust. Any level of society requires some agreement of common purpose which it would be impossible to carry out unless people agreed not to be unjust to one another. However, the fact that some form of justice in general is necessary for the survival of a social group does not mean that particular forms of injustice might not occur. Everyone might formally subscribe to the rules that make a society possible but one or two may from time to time exempt themselves from obedience. This might put them at a tremendous advantage in relation to individuals who always did the social thing. Take for instance a deviant state in international society that officially subscribes to the notion that disputes should be resolved peacefully. While relying on the compliance of other states to this rule it might well gain advantage by discretely threatening the use of force. In this way the calculating individual (or state) can always be at an advantage in relation to the just partner. This is referred to in the study of economics as the *'free rider problem'*. People who do not pay their fare, or steal from supermarkets, if they are successful, gain at the expense of others. It seems that the only answer to this problem is *compulsion*. The community member who intends to break the rules must be put in the position where the costs of doing so are greater than the advantages to be gained.

Plato sees this problem as tied up with the notion of human dignity. He suggests that the characteristic virtue of human beings is justice. The proper foundation of life is the mind. Through the proper employment of the intellect we can discover the nature of justice. So the use of justice is consonant with life.

Plato thinks the *Republic* should be founded on the basis of the division of labour. Essentially there are three types of people to be found in the society. There are those of a practical or business disposition who can get on with the work of providing in agriculture, trade and manufacture the basic needs of the community. Such people he sees as having souls of bronze or iron. At the next level are to be found more intelligent individuals who are strong and courageous. Their job is to look after the defence of the community; they have souls of silver. Third, there are the most intelligent members of the community who are most proficient at the most abstract forms of learning of which mathematics and philosophy are notable examples. Such people have souls of gold and it is they who rule the community. Plato calls members of the last two classes Guardians.

The Guardians

The Guardians are to live a life of austere simplicity. The aim of their existence must be the well-being of the state. They have to be housed and their material welfare has to be looked after in such a way that there is little opportunity for their interest to be taken up other than by concerns of the state. Plato believes they should have 'no private property beyond the barest essentials'.[9] They should be limited to a few personal possessions absolutely necessary for their existence. If they are to have the use of a dwelling-house or other property this should not be exclusively owned by any one of them. Property, in other words, must be held in common.

Plato stresses this because he thinks private property can become a divisive factor within society. If Guardians acquire (private) property in land, houses or money, they will become farmers and business people instead of Guardians, and 'harsh tyrants instead of partners in dealing with their own citizens'.[10] It would be fatal for the Guardians to share the same preoccupations of those over whom they rule. They would be one competing interest in the economic world possessing the exceptional advantage that they would have political power to carry out their material aims. The Guardians, therefore 'alone of all the citizens are forbidden to touch or handle silver or gold'.[11] Plato expressly wants to deprive the Guardians of personal material wealth so that they can be free to concentrate on the well-being of the community as a whole. Material interests should be left to the business and agricultural group. Nothing should be allowed to detract from the effectiveness of the ruling group in society.

Plato sees it as an improper objection to claim that his *Republic* would deprive the Guardians of everything which makes an ordinary man happy. The Guardians do their work for their keep only, they have no holidays, and have no money to spend on women. It may well be that the Guardians will not be happy as a result of the work they do. But 'our purpose in founding our state was not to promote the happiness of a single class, but, so far as is possible, of the whole community.'[12] The Guardians have to suffer one other important privation for the sake of the community as a whole. They are not allowed to have *wives or spouses*. All women must be held in common among members of the Guardian class.

These restrictions on the ownership of private property do not, of course, apply to the other classes of society. Private property is to be allowed in the industrial and agricultural classes. Plato would like to see the family dissolved (for the Guardian class). This does not mean Plato had in mind only an inferior status for women. His reason for wishing to break up the household or the family is because it sets *private* interest against public interest within the *Republic*. Plato is as much in favour of the equality of women with men as their differing qualities allow. Plato thinks that the only way to secure a genuine community of interest is to abolish all institutions which have on them the imprint of private interest. Women for him are inferior to men only in one respect, namely they do not share the same physical strength as them. Otherwise women should 'share the duties of men' and men and women can be used for the same purpose by the *Republic*.

Getting rid of inequality of the sexes and marriage in the Guardian class leaves Plato with the problem as to how sexual relations and the bringing up of children should be regulated. Plato starts from the premise that 'no parent should know his child or child his parent'.[13] Mating must be subject to strict regulations so that the best results might be achieved.

> We must, if we are to be consistent, and if we are to have a real pedigree 'herd', mate the best of our men with the best of our women as often as possible, and the inferior men with the inferior women as seldom as possible, and keep only the offspring of the best.[14]

Here Plato seems to get carried away in his enthusiasm for the community. There is much to object to in Plato's views from a modern point of view. His proposal for breeding in the Guardian class recalls the worst features of twentieth-century totalitarian regimes. We must bear in mind that 2,000 years have elapsed since the establishment of the *Republic*. But Plato's ideas did not go unchallenged in the classical world. Aristotle, in particular, objected to his proposals concerning marriage and private property. Aristotle was once, of course, a pupil of Plato so it was not a light matter for him to take objection to his ideas.

In order to be properly selected and then subsequently to defend and rule the state the Guardian class has to go through an extensive educational process. Plato feels that there are truths about life and society that can be learned through abstract study. Political theory can be put into practice in a most dramatic and comprehensive way in the ideal state. But

> the society we have described can never grow into a reality or see the light of day and there will be no end to the troubles of states or . . . of humanity itself, till philosophers become kings in this world, or till those we now call kings or rulers really and truly become philosophers, and political power and philosophy thus come into the same hands.[15]

One of the main features of world politics in the twentieth century has been the totalitarian form of government. Under a totalitarian government all aspects of human life become subject to the scrutiny and control of the authorities. Even the most minor activities become subject to the observation of those in charge. The clothes one wears, the acquaintances and friends one makes and, above all, the opinions one expresses become matters of public concern. And this public concern is backed up by a comprehensive police system and possibly an informal system of spying. Under a totalitarian system nothing one does is above suspicion: there is no such thing as an innocent act.

Examples of societies where it is generally agreed the totalitarian form of rule has sprung into existence are Nazi Germany, Mussolini's Italy, Stalinist Russia, Maoist China and countries of the presently dissolving eastern bloc. It is sometimes suggested that Third World countries which are rapidly industrializing, such as Taiwan and South Korea, have also adopted totalitarian forms of rule. Totalitarianism is often contrasted with the liberal or open system of government typified perhaps by the United States, Britain or Canada.

Karl Popper is a writer who gave currency to the concept of totalitarianism and in particular the contrast between the open and closed society. In a two-volume book entitled *The Open Society and its Enemies* (published in 1945) he defended the western liberal form of government from its Marxist and Fascist detractors. It is to Plato that he attributes a great deal of the blame for the rise of totalitarian ideas. He argues that Plato in *The Republic* develops a view of society which prejudices an open democratic style of government. He feels that Plato rules out social experimentation, individual initiative and piecemeal social and political reform in the treatise. Instead he sees Plato as presenting a recipe for success in politics drawing on a distinctive view of knowledge. Popper dislikes the way in which Plato confines knowledge and insight to a philosophical elite and he finds even more alarming Plato's suggestion that it is this philosophical elite that should rule society. In a colourful passage Popper describes Plato as 'a totalitarian party politician, unsuccessful in his immediate and practical undertakings, but in the long run only too successful in his propaganda for the arrest and overthrow of a civilization which he hates'.[16]

What lies behind the totalitarian vision is the notion that one individual or group of individuals can know what is best for society. We are all inclined to think that we are correct in what we believe, but what the totalitarian does is to conclude that his belief must apply to the beliefs of others as well. Popper thinks this error is exhibited in a most glaring way in Plato's political philosophy. The impact of totalitarianism on world society has been enormous. Those who have been totalitarian leaders at home have tended to be totalitarian leaders abroad. Hitler sought to impose his vision of the perfect Aryan race, with disastrous consequences, upon Europe. Stalin found no great difficulty in trying to export his totalitarian order from the Soviet Union to eastern Europe. Totalitarian leaders have felt that they have the answer to the problems of human society and have felt no reticence about indiscriminately exporting this answer to other societies.

Plato, according to Popper, sets this arrogance on its way. 'Inherent in Plato's programme there is a certain approach towards politics which is most dangerous. The Platonic approach I have in mind can be described as that of utopian engineering.'[17] This approach sets forward a blueprint for society as a whole, and 'is one which demands a strong centralized rule of a few, and which therefore is likely to lead to a dictatorship.'[18]

Popper regards Plato as taking a holist approach to politics and society. By this Popper means that Plato does not deal with social issues on the basis of their individual merits but rather in terms of an overall 'blanket' approach. With Plato, seemingly, social phenomena are seen in terms of one unifying standpoint. In the case of *The Republic* this unifying standpoint is the good of the society as a whole. Popper doubts if any such general notion of justice can be discovered, certainly not one that would cover national and world society. In fact Popper believes that the search for such a unifying vision can only be dangerous and the intent to implement it disastrous. Popper traces this totalitarian vision through from Plato to Hegel and Marx. Marxism for Popper is the dreadful realization of Plato's holist vision. These are the strong words with which Popper dismisses Plato:

> with all his uncompromising canvas-cleaning, [Plato] was led along a path on which he compromised his integrity with every step he took. He was forced to combat free thought, and the pursuit of truth. He was led to defend lying, political miracles, tabooistic superstition, the suppression of truth, and ultimately, brutal violence.... Excellent as Plato's sociological diagnosis was, his own development proves that the therapy he recommended is worse than the evil he tried to combat'.[19]

Plato veers to the extreme of seeking explanation and truth even if it leads to uncomfortable practical conclusions. He takes the Socratic view that knowledge is virtue and allows for no break between thinking and acting. Given this disposition what is Plato's attitude to the conduct of politics? Politics for Plato involves the pursuit of justice. Justice is a universally applicable concept which is not therefore coloured by considerations of time or place. We can see from the concepts of justice that Plato rejects, how he sees this is so.

The first notions of justice that he rejects concern the personal attributes of individuals. As we have seen, he will not accept that being honest in word and deed, and giving every person their due represents justice. The problem with such personal characteristics is that their evaluation is personal as well. The honest act is not always appreciated as such and, indeed, in one context an honest act can appear dishonest. Plato feels that justice cannot be tied down to any particular act. For instance it may appear just always to act fairly toward individuals. This may require that resources be shared out in an equal way. But where one individual or state is poor and another is rich, the equal apportionment of extra wealth may appear as great unfairness. The rich state or individual will simply be adding to their already advantaged position.

We can see here how Plato's deliberations on justice connect with the conduct of politics. The conduct of politics involves appropriate political action. In seeking to govern successfully we may like to find a helpful set of rules to fall back on. If justice is possible in individual and interstate relations it may appear that such a set of rules must be available for us to employ. But what Plato alerts us to is that this may not necessarily be the case.

This point is brought home in Plato's discussion of Thrasymachus's view of justice in *The Republic*. Thrasymachus's view of justice is that it consists always of the right of the stronger party. Whoever rules, therefore, dictates the nature of justice. This conclusion may appear to coincide with the current structure of international politics. In the modern world international law appears not to be too firmly founded and disputes are apparently ultimately soluble only through the use of force. Thrasymachus's cynical view would appear correct. But Plato rejects this view because it rests on an indefinable view of the interests of the stronger party. Are those who belong to the stronger party always sure where their best interests lie? It would seem to know if they are pursuing justice (and their own interest) that these rulers must have a very precise knowledge of their interests and needs.

In knowledge then, for Plato, lies the clue to justice. To know how to conduct political affairs, both national and international, a political leader should, for Plato, have a sound grasp of philosophy. The main focus of philosophy for Plato is on the theory of knowledge and ethics.

What is interesting about Plato's view of knowledge is that he sees it as objective and certain. Indeed, so certain is he of its nature that he speaks of 'forms' which pre-date the world and human existence. The world and human existence merely allow these forms to embody themselves. Thus for the concepts we employ in social and political life such as peace, law, justice, property and war there exists the perfect form which the philosopher can outline. On the whole, Plato believes there is but one way in which justice can correctly be viewed and consequently the best political order established and maintained. Plato feels that he may have the one correct prescription for society.

Plato's vision of political conduct

The leaders of states want to survive and prosper in the international context. To survive successfully they need an appropriate and applicable view of the context of politics.

Plato's view of how politics should be conducted is tied closely to his view of knowledge. He argues that the ideal political system will not be achieved until philosophers are rulers and rulers philosophers. He outlines a rigorous training for these philosopher rules in *The Republic*. This rigorous training, primarily in theoretical disciplines but to a lesser extent also in the physical disciplines, is not complete until the would-be leader is in his or her middle age.

Maturity plays a role in good government for Plato but this is not seen most forcibly in terms of emotional or biological maturity but rather in terms of intellectual maturity. For Plato it is the capacity to reason which makes one most suited to rule. Then one may be in a position to carry out the plans envisaged by philosophical insight for society. Political theory has one of its strongest, if not its wisest, advocates in Plato. With Plato theorists would dictate the conduct of policy. The nearest such a position has been attained in practice is in Leninist politics where the party ideologist has also been the party leader.

Plato aims for rationalization in his theory of state. The society is taken without regard to tradition – indeed, there is a strong effort to break from tradition in instituting the most severe censorship – an attempt is made to force it into a mould which coincides with Plato's vision of justice.

Plato's vision of justice is a society where each is directed to the activity they are best at. We might imagine this at the international level with each separate state being directed to produce those goods and specialize in those activities at which they excel. Plato's assumption with regard to individuals is that they are born with certain aptitudes and capacities and the most suitable life for individuals is to devote themselves exclusively to activities which draw on their natural aptitudes. In a society where everyone is engaged in this way the maximum will be achieved from everyone and this will contribute most to the well-being of the individual.

Plato even goes so far as to assume that each individual can be made to believe a myth which accords to them a different variety of soul. Some have souls of gold, some have souls of silver and the majority of souls are iron or bronze. People fit into different slots in a society according to the nature of their souls. Since people have no choice about their aptitudes, what results is an easily governed society where one of the main tasks for the rulers is to ensure that individuals are engaged in the activities best suited to their abilities.

One of the major problems with Plato's approach can be seen most readily if we see his notion of justice and specialization in an interstate context. In an interstate system where each society was required to devote itself to that activity at which it excelled, there would be little opportunity for development and change. In a word, the system would not be dynamic. The same can be said about Plato's vision of justice in relation to individuals. There appears to be no room for individuals to alter and develop their characters in the course of their lives.

Plato believes that there are straightforward answers to the problems of political life. If we think about such problems sufficiently – apply the best brains to them – then we shall get the right answer. We can see this in his allegory of the cave. Social life he would regard as obscure to the participants because they are achieved by their preconceptions and habits. But this is not so for the philosopher.

Once the individual – through philosophical insight – breaks away from those chains, the sunlight can be observed. The light of truth should (for Plato) guide us in our practical life. However, things are not as simple as this. If we can see Plato's philosophical vision in the context of international life some difficulties become apparent. Rulers who followed Plato's vision would believe themselves to have found the truth – to which others ought necessarily adhere. They could command the obedience of their subjects and also tyrannize the international community. In the name of truth, the most awesome blunders might be made. The knowledge of one individual is probably always partial and incomplete. Similarly those governing a state have a limited and partial view of their state and world society. A Platonic approach which assumes the truth is apparent to all rational persons can lead only to conflict. Not even philosophers have a monopoly on the truth.

Notes

1. M.B. Foster (1969) *Masters of Political Thought*, vol. 1, London: Harrap, p. 31.
2. Plato (1972) *The Republic*, Harmondsworth: Penguin, pp. 51–63.
3. *The Republic*, pp. 669–72.
4. *The Republic*, p. 107.
5. *The Republic*, p. 108.
6. *The Republic*, p. 182.
7. *The Republic*, p. 182.
8. *The Republic*, p. 196.
9. *The Republic*, p. 162.
10. *The Republic*, p. 163.
11. *The Republic*, p. 163.
12. *The Republic*, p. 164.
13. *The Republic*, p. 212.
14. *The Republic*, pp. 214–15.
15. *The Republic*, p. 233.
16. K. Popper (1977) *The Open Society and its Enemies*, vol. 1, London: Routledge, p. 169.
17. *The Open Society and its Enemies*, vol. 1, p. 157.
18. *The Open Society and its Enemies*, vol. 1, p. 159.
19. *The Open Society and its Enemies*, p. 200.

Further reading

Annas, J. (1981) *An Introduction to Plato's Republic*, Oxford: Oxford University Press.
Cross, R.C. and Woozley, A.D. (1964) *Plato's Republic*. London: Macmillan.
Neu, J. (1971) 'Plato's analogy of state and individual: The Republic and the organic theory of the state', *Philosophy* **46**: 238–54.
Nicholson, P.P. (1974) 'Unravelling Thrasymachus's arguments in the Republic', *Phronesis* **19**: 210–32.
Plato (1972) *The Republic*, Harmondsworth: Penguin.
Popper, K. (1977) *The Open Society and its Enemies*, London: Routledge.
Sinclair, T.A. (1971) *A History of Greek Political Thought*, London: Routledge.
White, N.P. (1979) *A Companion to Plato's Republic*, Oxford: Basil Blackwell.

2 | ARISTOTLE: PRACTICAL WISDOM AND THE BEST STATE

Aristotle was born in Stagira, northern Greece, at the beginning of the 99th Olympiad, 85 years after the death of Socrates and 384 years before the birth of Christ. Aristotle's family was extremely wealthy; a great deal of this wealth was inherited by Aristotle when his parents died in his early youth. Members of his family were prominent in the public life of the city and Aristotle himself is reputed to have played a prominent part in the civic life of his birthplace. His reputation as a philosopher brought fame and good fortune to Stagira.

At the age of 17 Aristotle travelled to Athens where he joined Plato's Academy. Very soon he became one of Plato's leading students. Plato is reputed to have remarked that Aristotle was the 'soul of his school' and in Aristotle's absence from the Academy Plato is supposed to have said that his lectures had fallen on 'deaf ears'.[1] There seems little doubt that Aristotle was Plato's outstanding pupil.

Aristotle's prodigious output throughout his life and his extraordinary contribution to human knowledge are testimony to his great energy and intellect. He seems to have surpassed Plato in his industry and scope of inquiry. Aristotle contributed decisively to ethics, politics, economics, biology and physics. He was a genuinely universal scholar. Possibly, however, his greatest achievement may lie in the field of logic. In his *Prior and Posterior Analytics* and his *Metaphysics* he virtually founded the subject and still today provides the basis for the teaching of formal logic.

One further fact of Aristotle's eventful life deserves notice: he is said to have acted as tutor to Alexander the Great of Macedon. If this is true, and there is strong evidence to show that it might be so, it is difficult to imagine a more remarkable combination of intellect and political leadership. Alexander went on to establish a great Empire and Aristotle became one of the world's foremost philosophers. The acquaintance with Alexander may also account for the realism with which Aristotle approaches his task in the study of politics.

On one visit to the United States President Gorbachev of the Soviet Union is supposed to have remarked that he felt very 'much at home there' and added 'we all want the good life'. Here Gorbachev, perhaps unwittingly, echoed the sentiments of Aristotle. Because for Aristotle the objective of political science is the 'good for man' and he defined this as the 'good life'.

For Aristotle many things combine to produce the good life. In the first place humans have to have a disposition to act virtuously if they are to enjoy the good life, but this in itself is not enough. There belongs to the good life also an element of material well-being and good fortune. No one who is poor, ugly or maimed can entirely enjoy the good life. Possibly this is what Gorbachev had in mind when he spoke of the United States, which enjoyed the kind of prosperity that allowed it to offer its citizens the greatest variety of opportunities. But wealth is not all within Aristotle's perspective; equally no one who is entirely without virtue can experience the good life as well. The good life has to do with both means and ends. Happiness derives from pursuing the good in the right way. Were humans of a divine disposition contemplation would be the highest form of life, but they also have earthly wants, so contemplative activity has to give way to action.

Mulgan has suggested that arising from the objective of the good life the main political demands that Aristotle's political philosophy raises are for security and stability.[2] In contrast to modern political philosophers like Rousseau and Marx, Aristotle does not promote a conception of active citizenship. Involvement in political life is not necessary for the individual's happiness. The study of politics for Aristotle is not then aimed primarily at the educated public but rather at the statesman. This implies that Aristotle might have a great deal to teach the student of international relations at least as the subject has been classically taught. In both international history and in strategic studies the emphasis is very much on the nature and limitations of statesmanship.

Aristotle placed a great deal of stress upon the development of practical wisdom. The best statemanship derived not only from knowledge of the right ideas (as Plato appeared to imply in *The Republic*) but also from a sound practical understanding as to how to implement them. Such practical wisdom could not be learned through mere intellectual contemplation but had to be gathered from life itself. Good statesmanship was not possible without sound experience.

Plato gave his attention on the whole to the creation of an ideal state. In *The Republic* Plato suggests how a just society might be brought into being starting from scratch. Aristotle is more prepared, in contrast, to take states as they are and devise forms of ruling which might be successful.[3] There is a greater air of realism (it might be said) about Aristotle's approach.

This is not just a difference of approach, it has also to do with differences in methods of inquiry. Plato stressed a dialectical approach to political philosophy which went beyond much of common understanding. Aristotle is less inclined to depart from ordinary conceptions. In what he recommends, therefore, in political life he is more prepared to adhere to tradition, habit and custom. In *The Republic* Plato feels that he has a prescription which would apparently render the world harmonious overnight. Aristotle believes that the relations of individuals within states and the relations of states with one another are less susceptible to such immediate improvement. We have to work with what we have and not what we imagine to be the best state of affairs. Aristotle holds 'it clearly impossible that the knowledge of the wisest ruler can be better than the customary law'.[4] The rigid distinction between nature and convention, with the

> 'extreme intellectualism or rationalism to which this definition had committed Socrates and Plato, was thus broken down by Aristotle. *The reason of the statesman in a good state cannot be detached from the reason embodied in the law and custom of the community he rules.*'[5]

In other words, we have to expect diversity in politics and the interstate system.

Like Plato, Aristotle strongly believes that some individuals are a good deal more intelligent than others and, indeed, that a few enjoy entirely superior intelligence. However, superior intelligence does not imply that an individual has nothing to learn from the mass. Although individuals taken separately may be less intelligent, the combined intelligence of a number of individuals may well in its perceptiveness outweigh the insight of one individual. The product of collective wisdom should not be lightly dismissed. Even the wisest people have something to learn from their environment and the common person.

Aristotle's ethics favours the mean, often described as the golden mean; his politics is consequently one of moderation. The object is to bend nature, which includes both the society and the physical world, to our ends. That something is old and well-established should not imply a presumption against it. Tradition is not without its justification. Given this view it is not surprising that Aristotle holds that politics is not for the young. As Leo Strauss writes in his book *The City and Men*, 'Because the city as a whole is characterised by a specific recalcitrance to reason it requires for its well-being a rhetoric different from forensic and deliberative rhetoric as a servant to the political art'. On the basis of Aristotle's account of politics Strauss sounds the warning that 'the very nature of public affairs often defeats reason'.[6] Intellect in itself is not always sufficient to deal with a political and diplomatic problem.

Aristotle is, then, the philosopher of common sense. With any problem – intellectual or practical – his response is, first of all, to look at the problem more closely and then to divide the problem into its constituent parts. As befits the founder of natural science and logic Aristotle takes an analytical approach and this is to be seen in his conception of politics. Statemanship can be learned through a combination of experiment and study. The only possible laboratory in political science and international relations is life itself: we have to observe from our experience which policies are successful and under what circumstances.

Nature and function

When we first come to study international politics there is, I think, a sense in which the international system seems as it ought to be. That Britain is in NATO, a member of the European Community and that the United States is a liberal democracy, also a member of NATO and has close economic ties with its neighbour Canada seems about correct. The world order seems *natural* and appears equally natural for us to accept it as such. After all, the present arrangements have grown from thousands of years of history and the acceptance of culture and practices. As Aristotle puts it: 'It follows that the state belongs to a class of objects which exist in nature and that man is by nature a political animal; it is his nature to live in a state'.[7] The world seems functional as it is. As we progress in our studies of international politics some may come to challenge this view, others, however, may legitimately feel that the 'naturalist' gets it about right.

Aristotle would endorse this 'naturalistic' view. Everything in nature and society has its function or purpose for Aristotle. Things are as they are by design. He begins his *Politics* with the observation that 'every state is an association of persons formed with a view to some good purpose'.[8] Thus all states have a rationale of their own, ordained by nature. One of his first analyses in the work is intended to demonstrate that slavery (which was the norm in Greek society) was an institution which was natural and just. Tools for Aristotle were necessary for survival and slaves 'were animate tools'.[9] There is a place for the slave in the order of things, and as humans have been endowed by nature with different qualities, some with intelligence and others only with sound bodily qualities, it is perfectly fitting that the unintelligent but industrious should be slaves. But they are tools in a positive and cared-for sense as part of the master's body.[10]

Just as slavery is natural, so also is the household. And what is natural is good. Aristotle criticizes Plato for wanting to do away with the family in the Guardian class, for this would undermine valuable affections and interests. Aristotle finds great worth in the type of household common among the Greeks. This household was slightly more extensive than the modern one in that it was also a productive unit. The slaves were owned by the household and they provided for the unit's physical needs through their agricultural labour. So for Aristotle the family is the key productive and reproductive unit in society. Not only is it the proper place for rearing children and providing them but also it plays a vital social role in introducing children to the morality of the community.

Thus, in Aristotle's view, Plato undermines much that is good in suggesting that property and wives should be held in common. He does not share Plato's assumption that the ownership of private property leads to endless disputes among individuals. Indeed he thinks common ownership is just as likely to give rise to dispute. Undermining private ownership will also jeopardize the pride that individuals naturally derive from ownership. Having something as your own, Aristotle thinks, can in itself give rise to an immense amount of pleasure. We love what is ours just as we love ourselves. Equally we can learn to love ourselves in loving what we have. A great deal is gained by allowing individuals to own things themselves. We can be more confident that something will be looked after if it is owned. Common possession is, then, contrary to human nature. Plato prevents entirely natural ethical relations between mother and child, father and son, father and daughter, husband and wife coming into being. As these natural ethical relations are often the basis of wider social morality, Plato risks the community as a whole when he seeks to undermine the family and private property in the Guardian class.

It is interesting to speculate as to what Aristotle's reaction would be to the collapse of communism in eastern Europe. Probably Aristotle would have held that those states were founded on an unworkable concept of property. The common ownership in the means of production which Marxism-Leninism encouraged would, from Aristotle's perspective, lead to an indifference towards the means for sustaining economic life. Since the factories and the land in eastern Europe belonged to no one in particular there would be no reason to show interest in them. If economic advance were a product of collective ownership this would be achieved at the expense of a sense of identification with the institutions which created the wealth. Aristotle might not have been surprised to note that alienation from society was a pervasive feature of life in eastern Europe under communism.

A similar approach to the international order would see the nation-state as natural. The diversity and internal harmony of linguistic and ethnic groups might be seen from an Aristotelian standpoint as contributing to a vibrant world order. But there is both a strength and a flaw in this argument about naturalness. Existing human institutions cannot, it seems, have come into being without fulfilling some need. The international order as it stands has its merits. But we are all also aware that no human order persists without change. Slavery is no longer regarded as natural. There must be some way in which Aristotle's functional order can pass from what is natural today to what is natural tomorrow. There is an in-built tendency apparently towards conservatism in Aristotle's view of statecraft.

For the Aristotelian the object at which international theory might aim would be the good of the international system. Since it is difficult to discern in which respect the international system forms an entity in its own right Aristotelians might possibly regard the good at which the system aims as being the good of the individual states which form the system. Individuals within states are not so fortunate, however. The good of the individual is subordinate to the good of the state – however much the individual is worth. Statesmen should have some knowledge of psychology[11] in order to make their fellow citizens good people and obedient to the laws. 'Now matters of conduct and considerations of what is to our advantage have no fixity about them any more than matters affecting our health'. We need to aim at the mean 'between excess and deficiency'.[12]

Aristotle's advice to political leaders reflects his belief in the functional nature of existing institutions: there is no magic formula with which to deal with political problems. An educated elite such as Plato's Guardian class is no more likely to get things right than the presently established ruler. Aristotle notes that in practical life knowledge cannot be as precise as we might expect it to be in the natural sciences. We have to operate with the precision with which the material allows. Human action is unpredictable – even if it is patterned. There is therefore an element of hit or miss in the practical doctrines – both in ethics and politics – that we devise.

In the light of the possible errors of our thinking Aristotle recommends a balanced approach to political leaders. They – just as the individual in everyday life – should aim at the golden mean. They should not lean too much towards one interpretation of events. In deciding upon policy leaders should avoid extremes and where possible they should build on past practice. Great inequalities in wealth within a society should, for instance, be avoided. And often in bringing a stability to a constitution a mixture of the opposite element – such as aristocracy within a democracy – may well produce beneficial effects.

In dealing with conflict statesmen have to aim at 'the voluntary act preceded by deliberation' (proairesis). Statesmen are involved a great deal in deliberation, which Aristotle defines as

> things which while in general following certain definite lines, have no predictable issues, or the result of which cannot be clearly stated, or in which, when important decisions have to be made, we take others into our counsels, distorting our own abilities to settle the point.[13]

Prudence and the good life

Prudence is the exact opposite of intuitive intelligence: it comes with age. You can be a good mathematician in your youth but you cannot demonstrate 'proairesis' until later life. Profound knowledge does not allow you to deliberate well.[14] Aristotle's advice for the leader is to act quickly, think slowly. Results demonstrate the excellence of one's deliberative qualities – but they must be results in the right regard.

In his book *Aristotle on Equality and Justice* W. von Leyden argues that for Aristotle 'the common people tend to become mutinous if the distribution of property is unequal, whereas men of taste and refinement might revolt if the distribution of offices or honours is equal'. So 'the causes of insurrection always lie in a difference of interpretation of the nature of justice and equality'.[15] In arguments about justice there is seemingly no clear-cut answer. People see justice differently. They do not accept the Platonic view of one objective justice and this is what leads to revolt. As a consequence, no constitution is perfectly adapted for every possible set of circumstances. Societies are varied in their composition and so their political institutions will vary. This might seem to leave Aristotle without a general policy to recommend. But what prevents him from losing his thread altogether is his belief in the excellence of nature. Variety and complexity are in keeping with nature and as justice is itself natural the task of statesmen is to bring out the order inherent in their circumstances. As Morrall puts it, there are 'natural virtues which make men act in accordance with right reason'. There are also 'relative impulses which serve the development of man's natural politics'.[16] So practical reason can discover what is good for us.

The question as to what is the best kind of state to guarantee international peace is one that is extremely difficult to answer; this has not prevented the question from arising. At the beginning of the 1990s, as old regimes are swept away in eastern Europe, this is a problem which arises acutely. Those who have to create a new order are highly conscious of the international dimensions of the problems with which they deal. The Czechoslovak leader, Vaclav Havel, sees progress within his country as depending on the undermining of the two-bloc system. And the appearance of a new German state depends upon the existence of an adequate international dimension to the unification plan.

A problem which concerned Aristotle which is closely allied to this issue of what is the best political system to ensure peace, is the question of what constitutes the best kind of state in itself. It seems to me unlikely that we are going to have an adequate answer to the first question of a peaceful state without having a reasonably successful answer to the second. A state which fails to hold together internally is also one that will fail to contribute to a working international order.

In line with his general political philosophy which commends diversity Aristotle has a number of responses to the issue. His advice mostly has a conservative tinge to it. Policy for Aristotle has to follow the golden mean.

> In all states there are three sections of the community: the very well-off, the very badly-off and those in between. Seeing therefore that it is

agreed that moderation and a middle position are best, it is clear that in the matter of possessions to own a middling amount is best of all.[17]

But it is not clear from Aristotle's account for whom this is the best. Is it best for oneself to be in the middle rank or is it best for the society? According to Aristotle it is difficult for the rich and well off to follow reason since they already have so many of the good things in life: equally it is difficult for the downtrodden and the poor since they have to do without so much. The rich 'commit deeds of violence on a large scale, the latter are delinquent and wicked in petty ways'.[18] The misdeeds of one class are due to hubris, the misdeeds of the other to rascality. *Hubris* is insolent pride or security which might lead the rich to arrogance and overconfidence. Yet perversely it is the middle section of society that for Aristotle is best suited to govern that least wants to hold office.

When those who are anxious to rule – from among the poor and the well off – do so the result is a state not of 'free man but of slaves and master, the one full of envy, the other of contempt'. This is the worst of all worlds: 'nothing could be farther removed from friendship or from the whole idea of a shared partnership in a state'.[19] In the best form of state ruling is regarded as a common task, not to be carried out by all, but in which all feel they have a part. A state without such an atmosphere of friendship will find it difficult to govern. 'Sharing is a token of friendship; one does not share even a journey with people one does not like'.[20]

For Aristotle it is 'clear then that the political partnership which operates through the middle is best'.[21] One problem a statesman adopting Aristotle's approach in practice might have is establishing who in fact constitutes the middle rank. Membership varies from society to society and changes over time. Equally people of the middle rank may not themselves be free of envy and contempt. It is only in a society that is fully static that membership of the middle rank will be easily discerned.

Aristotle's notion of effective government is most interesting. In my view a balanced and successful international order can be attained only where individual states are effectively ruled. A badly governed state, like Nazi Germany, is likely to have poor relations with its neighbours. Effective government is a partnership. Friendship is essential to make the relationship work well. Leaders drawn from the middle will not induce hostility from other ranks in society. James Mill followed a similar line of argument in his 'Essay on Government' which was influential in the movement which brought about the Great Reform Act of 1832.[22] Aristotle's view might lead us to argue that power in Third World states might now best fall into the hands of the middle class. But in Third World states it might be that people are either absorbed into the modern economy and extremely rich or in the native section and extremely poor. Following this line of reasoning we might expect only poor governments from states in this situation.

'In small states it is easy for the whole body to become divided into two, leaving no middle at all and they are nearly all rich or poor.'[23] So a middle form of constitution halfway between an oligarchy dominated by the rich and a democracy dominated by the poor will be the most successful. In order for a state to work you have first to ensure that the majority supports the constitution.[24] Where the middle sections of society are behind the constitution the rest of society may follow. The best possible situation is where the middle ranking are in a majority, but if this is not possible it is at least desirable the middle ranking are more numerous than the rich and the poor taken singly. There is a certain timeless quality about the advice that Aristotle offers. It might be thought that non-capitalist societies may not suffer from the inequalities and problems Aristotle discusses. But the experience of the Soviet Union and eastern Europe seems to suggest that even in socialist societies it is important to ensure that it is not only the really well off which dominates.

Of the two groups in society, Aristotle most fears the domination of the rich. 'The successful power-grabbing of the rich does more harm to society than lust for power in the people'.[25] So the mean at which Aristotle aims may induce stability. He sets himself the task of establishing an equilibrium in society. But this might not necessarily always be what is needed. Successful societies may be those that adapt and change most rapidly. The extreme might be the most attractive proposition under certain circumstances. If we return to the societies of eastern Europe, what they most require seems not to be stability which might involve a return to totalitarian forms of rule: they need to evolve most rapidly beyond their previous point of equilibrium.

Ellen and Neal Wood's assessment of Aristotle as a natural conservative and realist seems to be an accurate one.[26] Aristotle appears to be fond of hierarchy and this hierarchy corresponds to the level of birth that a person enjoys. An Aristotelian view of the world would tend towards a pragmatic acceptance of previously attained states of affair. While Aristotle seems not to be a racist, he might none the less accept divisions of advantages which occurred among nations of different racial backgrounds. Aristotle favours what works and has a suspicion of excessive innovation. He is anxious that political leaders should not overreach themselves and seek to bend social situations and political relations beyond what they might not tolerate. Aristotle perhaps earns his place as one of the first political realists, and if so one of the most profound.

Notes

1. E. Walford (1885) *The Politics and Economics of Aristotle*, London: George Bell, p. iv.
2. R.G. Mulgan (1977) *Aristotle's Political Theory*, Oxford: Oxford University Press, p. 7.

3. *Aristotle's Political Theory*, p. 97: Aristotle was much happier criticizing other people's ideal states than describing his own. His arguments also illustrate his deep mistrust of simple solutions.
4. G.H. Sabine and T.L. Thorson (1973) *A History of Political Theory*, Hinsdale, Ill: Holt-Sanders, p. 101.
6. L. Strauss (1978) *The City of Man*, Chicago, Ill: Chicago University Press, p. 22.
7. Aristotle (1970) *Politics*, Harmondsworth: Penguin, p. 28.
8. *Politics*, p. 25.
9. *Politics*, p. 31.
10. *Politics*, p. 36.
11. Aristotle (1970) *Ethics*, Harmondsworth: Penguin, p. 51.
12. *Ethics*, p. 66.
13. *Ethics*, pp. 84–6.
14. *Ethics*, pp. 182, 183.
15. W. von Leyden (1985) *Aristotle on Equality and Justice*, London: Macmillan, pp. 66, 68.
16. J.B. Morrall (1977) *Aristotle*, London: Allen & Unwin, p. 89.
17. *Politics*, p. 171.
18. *Politics*, p. 172.
19. *Politics*, p. 172.
20. *Politics*, p. 172.
21. *Politics*, p. 173.
22. See J. Rees and J. Lively (eds) (1978) *Utilitarian Logic and Politics*, Oxford: Oxford University Press.
23. *Politics*, p. 172.
24. *Politics*, p. 174.
25. *Politics*, p. 176.
26. E.M. Wood and N. Wood (1978) *Class Ideology and Ancient Political Theory*, Oxford: Basil Blackwell, pp. 209–37.

Further reading

Allan, D.J. (1952) *The Philosophy of Aristotle*, Oxford: Oxford University Press.
Aristotle (1970) *Ethics*, Harmondsworth: Penguin, especially books 1 and 4.
Aristotle (1970) *Politics*, Harmondsworth: Penguin, especially books 1 and 2.
Barker, E. (1906) *The Political Thought of Plato and Aristotle*, London: Methuen.
Huxley, G.L. (1985) 'On Aristotle's best state', *History of Political Thought*, vol VI (1/2): 139–50.
Irwin, T.H. (1985) 'Moral science and political theory in Aristotle', *History of Political Thought*, vol. VI (1/2): 150–69.
Johnson, C.N. (1990) *Aristotle's Theory of the State*, London: Macmillan.
Macintyre, A. (1985) *After Virtue*, London: Duckworth, especially ch. 12.
Morrall, J.B. (1977) *Aristotle*, London: Allen & Unwin.
Mulgan, R.G. (1977) *Aristotle's Political Theory*, Oxford: Oxford University Press.
Strauss, L. (1978) *The City and Man*, Chicago, Ill: Chicago University Press.
Wood, E.M. and Wood, N. (1978) *Class Ideology and Ancient Political Theory*, Oxford: Basil Blackwell.

3 | AUGUSTINE: THE FOUNDATIONS OF REALISM

An influential approach to the study of international politics has been that of the realist school. Those thinkers numbered among the realists are Max Weber, E.H. Carr, Hans Morgenthau, George Kennan and Henry Kissinger.[1] As the name suggests, realists take the view that international society has to be taken in its actual, sometimes brutal, context. Realists tend to see conflict as inherent in human life which they often see as governed by a struggle for power. They therefore advise caution in the setting of foreign policy goals and warn against the motives of rival states. One other theorist who can be legitimately regarded as belonging to this realist school is the theologian, Reinhold Niebuhr, who derives his stark view of interstate relations, governed as he sees them by the sin of pride, unashamedly from the Christian philosophical tradition. Niebuhr was highly influential in the United States for much of his later life. He helped shape the climate within which foreign policy was made. He believed strongly in the policy of containment pursued in relation to communism in the 1950s and 1960s. The view of humanity and society which formed a basis for Niebuhr's thinking is stated most clearly in Augustine's philosophy.

Niebuhr discusses Augustine in a seminal article entitled 'Augustine's political realism'. The article, which was first given as a public lecture, was published in 1953 at a period near the beginning of the Cold War when Niebuhr was establishing himself as a major influence upon American thinking. Niebuhr is most generous in his assessment of Augustine's thinking. He says of Augustine that he is, 'by general consent, the first great "realist" in Western history'.[2] Niebuhr defines realism, to which he ascribes, as a 'disposition to take all factors in a social and political situation, which offer resistance to established norms, into account, particularly the factors of self-interest and power'.[3] This realism Niebuhr distinguishes from an idealism which glosses over the imperfections of humans and neglects considerations of power. Niebuhr regards Augustine's political thinking as particularly appropriate to the American position of hegemonic power in the free world. Augustine's thinking leads one to stress the limitations of all political power and teaches those who exercise it to be wary of others who hold power. Niebuhr agrees with Augustine that corruption is never far below the surface in human society. This corruption does not have its root solely in humankind's animal nature but principally in the 'rational self'.[4] Thus no governmental power can be absolutely sanctified; some forms of political power are simply relatively less undesirable than others. Niebuhr sees in the Marxist pursuit of the perfect social and economic system a trap which threatens to undermine the whole of humanity. Niebuhr finds himself much more at home with Augustine's limited vision of the capabilities of human individuals. He joins with Augustine in believing that from human individuals in existing society a potential world community realizes itself only as a divine ideal.

Aristotle gives advice as to wise conduct both in politics and life. His advice is directed towards attaining the good life, and is based on the assumption that we can attain felicity in human and social interaction. With Aristotle there is an active interest in the political world and engagement in politics is seen as a fulfilling pursuit. The wise politician can improve human society and political theory can contribute to attaining this goal. With Aristotle our personal pursuit of ethical ends coincides with the politician's pursuit of the right objectives for the state. There is no ethical disharmony with Aristotle between public and private life, ethics, morality and politics.

One of the charms of ancient Greek life seems to be the simplicity with which moral and political problems are treated. Aristotle's 'naturalistic' doctrine appears to be an example of this simplicity. In being political animals we are doing right for ourselves as human actors. For us nowadays things are seemingly not so straightforward. Our personal morality might well, it seems, come into conflict with the requirements of the state. Our views on foreign policy may clash with those actually pursued by the state of which we are citizens. Many American writers in political theory and international relations found this was the case at the time of the Vietnam War. What the politician might from the 'ethical' standpoint of the state regard as a necessary action we might well deplore as a personal, moral action. But it seems difficult to get involved with politics, and particularly international politics and to take 'real' decisions, without in one way or another 'getting your hands dirty'. One reason why the apparent ease of the Aristotelian standpoint, where the ethical and political standpoint coincide, is not open to us is because other experiences and traditions have intervened since his time, foremost among those traditions is the Christian one, formidably represented in political theory by Augustine.

YEARY LIBRARY
LAREDO COMM. COLLEGE
LAREDO, TEXAS

In Greek society the individual lived the fullest life in concert with others. The city-state dominated the ethical outlook of the individual. It seems the biggest transformation which the rise of Christianity brought about in human reflection was connected with its stress on the individual. The dramatization of the life of Christ appears to draw attention to the uniqueness of each person. Personal salvation and social harmony might, it appears, be deeply at odds. Christian and, later, Stoic doctrine appears to offer a form of life which appeared to preserve the integrity of the individual in the face of the exigencies of fortune and political tension. The good life might not be found in the life of politics alone.

The *City of God,* Augustine's major work, took thirteen years to write.[5] The most important ideas of Augustine are those which centre round his doctrine of the 'two cities': *civitas dei* and *civitas terrena.* Michael Foster suggests that the doctrine of the *City of God* is derived from the Christian revelation which proclaims there is an everlasting life beyond this present life and also from the Roman philosopher Cicero's humanist notion of a society continuous with the universe which transcends all the limited associations of state, race, class and of which all people are qualified to be members by virtue of their common humanity.[6]

A theme of the *City of God* is the wretchedness of present life and its inability to offer us satisfactory moral inspiration. We have therefore to look beyond present life for our guidance: to a divine community which has everlasting qualities. Now although it was God's plan in the creation of the human race that all people should ultimately be members of this City of God, this plan was defeated by the fall. Since the fall, humans can become members of the Kingdom only by Grace, and since grace is not given to all, not all humans may become members. Potentially, however, any human being whatever may receive the grace of God.

One way of making easier our possible transition to the City of God is through becoming members of the Christian Church. The common love and worship of God has the consequence that the very act of worship makes the worshipper a member of one community. 'The members of the heavenly City', in a phrase which recurs many times, 'enjoy community with God and wth one another in God'.[7]

Although Augustine sometimes implies that the City of God and the Catholic Church are one and the same entity, it is clear that they are distinct. The City has a wider membership than the Church, since it includes both the good angels and the electorate who have departed from this life: the Church contains in its ranks some who are not members of the City. In other words, membership of the Church is not a guarantee that you are among the elect. The Church and the City of God cannot be coterminous since they inhabit different realms of time. The City of God is everlasting whereas the Church belongs to human time. None the less 'men can attain membership of the City only by the gift of grace, and the normal means of the conferment of grace are the sacraments of the Church'.[8] Thus although the Church belongs solely to the human realm it can still offer a point of orientation in the quest for the eternal city. As Foster puts it, 'The Church is both one section of the City, comprising those members who are still on their pilgrimage through the world, and the avenue through which all (or almost all) who are members of the City must have passed'.[9]

This religious viewpoint compares interestingly with Plato's pre-Christian position. For Plato justice can be realized in *The Republic*. The task of political philosophy and that of the good citizen are one and the same. Ethics and social life need not be in conflict with one another. Augustine opens the way to a realist view of politics and international relations. For Augustine

> there exists no justice in the absolute sense in the state as such. A state exists by imposing an order upon its members, and its strength and vigour depend upon the willingness and devotion with which they accept it. Its justice depends upon its conformity to the universal order, and the working state may well use its strength to infringe and violate this order.[10]

Absolute justice therefore only belongs to the universal order. But this universal order is not present in the world. To conform to the universal order is to obey the will of God, embodying a set of values beyond present-day society. Augustine counsels an acceptance of earthly imperfection and suggests that we abandon the notion of earthly community in the present yet preserve the notion of community as an ideal. Present political policy may then conflict with the ideal of a world community. Realism in international politics takes its starting-point from this divorce between the actual and the desirable.

The doctrine of the *City of Good* from the individual's point of view is no less gloomy. It suggests that he who is 'good is free, though he be a slave, and he that is evil, a slave though he be a King'.[11] Augustine's appeal is for individuals to transfer their ultimate allegiance from the state to the universal society, for which there exists no corresponding institutional order. However, making the distinction between the secular and the religious sphere and arguing that the state should be excluded from the latter morally, curiously backs up the earthly state. The existing state is reinforced in its authority since it seems Augustine's conclusion is that there can be no better society here. Thus although there can be no true morality in the here and now, Augustine nevertheless opens up the possibility of there being a partial morality of national interest.

War and peace

According to Augustine all humans strive towards peace, which is a natural law. He says: 'even thieves themselves that molest all the world besides them are at peace amongst themselves'.[12] Thus every society, earthly and heavenly alike, aims at peace. The two societies differ only in the kind of peace at which they aim. The former aims only at a society of human beings in ordered relations with one another; but the end of the latter is the peace of God, 'the most orderly and concordant partnership in the fruition of God and of one another in God'.[13]

As Augustine remarks, in the Christian ethos 'a man is commended to love his neighbour as his own self, so must he do for his wife, children, family and all men besides: thus shall be settled in peace and orderly concord with the world'.[14] And he is commended in his religion to seek to attain a universal peace. But such a 'world-order is not of course a system of states'.[15] A system of legal and political relationships is one thing, but there is more, for: *the highest kind of peace is considered a system united by the bond of love.*[16] Such love, extending beyond family and state to all people, is possible only to those who have the love of God. A system in which all people are actively united with one another by the love of one another in God, this is what Augustine means by universal peace. In contrast to this ideal, the earthly city is 'divided in itself into wars, altercations, and appetites of bloody and deadly victories'. Peace in the earthly city is paradoxically sought by 'laborious' war.[17] In terms both of the divine life and the life of humankind in the present the goal of peace appears to be a long way off. For Niebuhr it is this ideal of world community (however remote from the present world) which prevents the Augustinian account of politics from falling into cynicism.

In Augustine's view human life is at all levels extremely fragile and precarious. This again appeals to the realist Niebuhr.[18]

Human pride must take second place to this natural sense of vulnerability. Augustine sees human society as becoming progressively more perilous the larger and more impersonal it becomes. After the city or town 'comes the world, which the philosophers reckon as the third level of human society'.[19] The first two levels of human society are those of individual or family existence and social or communal existence in an ever more urban environment. This third level of human existence brings with it its own characteristics: 'the world being like a confluence of waters, is obviously more full of danger than the other communities because of its greater size'.[20] Augustine notes that at this level 'the diversity of languages separates man from man'. Where people cannot communicate their thoughts to each other through a common language fellowship is extra-ordinarily difficult. It may well be that 'a man would be more cheerful with his dog than with a foreigner'.[21]

Relations with other states are always therefore tricky. 'I shall be told that the Imperial City has been at pains to impose on conquered peoples not only her yoke but her language also, as a bond of peace and fellowship.'[22] Rome extended its influence in the international community in the only way possible by extending the borders of its language as well. Differences of language can be overcome by imposing one language. But Augustine has his doubts if conquest is justified: 'think of the cost of this achievement'.[23] Consider the scale of those wars which led to the subjugation of non-Roman peoples. A state can have no truly successful foreign policy.

For this reason war for Augustine is an enduring feature of human life. He seems to draw this bleak view from what he sees going on around him. Roman civilization had its great advantages but could only seemingly be sustained by conquest. Augustine seems to think that these aggressive wars were far harder to justify than wars that attempted to defend the empire once established. Misery and grief are the emotions that come to Augustine's mind when he speaks of wars. 'But the wise man, they say, will wage just wars'. However: 'Surely, if he remembers that he is a human being, he will rather lament the fact he is faced with the necessity of waging just wars; for if they were not just, he would not have to engage in them.'[24]

Despite these reservations about the waging of wars Augustine is often regarded as one of the founders of the Christian doctrine of a just war. The feelings of the early Christian fathers were seemingly against aggression and militant forms of self-defence. When attacked by an opponent the advice of the Gospels is to turn the other cheek. Augustine himself sees self-defence as an improper justification for attacking another. On the whole he favours passivity and stoicism in the individual, but he does not always extend this doctrine to the state. A state may justly wage a war where its own existence is threatened or the established order is placed in doubt. Although we cannot be sure that the existing world order is divinely sanctioned we can be sure that there is a relative temporal obligation to uphold whatever order exists.

A war then may be just in relation to the rules that govern human society. But war is never morally attractive. War can give rise to its own evils which can render unjust even the most just of causes. Augustine warns that no war should be waged simply from a love of violence or a lust for power.[25] Christians fight a war from necessity, not to give vent to their emotions; they will not then engage in war with innocent people nor prolong it more than is necessary.

Secular power is never wholly sanctified

'The peace which the earthly society secures is a good not only to the men who know no higher peace but also to the members of the City of God themselves, so long as they are pilgrims on earth.'[26] They need the security and order which it provides in order to be free from disturbance and molestation in the performance of their religious duties. They must, therefore, respect the laws by which this security is maintained and render obedience to the power by whom the laws are enforced. In respect of their willingness to obey they will not be distinguished from those who are citizens of the earthly society alone; they will differ from them only in the spirit with which their obedience is rendered.

However, Christians will render their obedience only to the secular authority within the limits of secular affairs.

> The Heavenly City observes and respects this temporal peace here on earth, and the coherence of men's wills in honest morality, as far as it may with a safe conscience; yes, and so far desires it, making use of it for the attainment of the actual peace.[27]

The goal of an everlasting peace takes precedence over the goal of present peace. Present peace is not neglected, but should be seen more as a means for the attainment of a larger goal.

Augustine's political theory teaches that we are not to expect too much from our present rulers. Any government is bound to be fallible and, more crucially, cannot escape the taint of evil. For Niebuhr this implies we cannot ever wholly put our faith in a system of government or its office-holders. Their power has to be subject to checks and balances. Niebuhr's deep suspicion of Soviet power in the early Cold War period was partially based on his assessment that under communist regimes power was not adequately checked.

Further evidence of Augustine's profound realism and pessimism about the human condition can be seen in his attitude to slavery. 'Sin, therefore, is the monitor of servitude, and first cause of man's subjection to man; which notwithstanding comes not to pass but by the direction of the highest, in whom is no injustice.'[28] We ourselves are responsible for our diminished condition. Even if the particular individual involved has done nothing to deserve her servitude, none the less the sins of humanity as a whole are sufficient to justify that particular servitude. There can be no justification for resisting our earthly masters.

> Therefore the apostle [Paul] warns servants to obey their masters and to serve them with cheerfulness, and good will: to the end that if they cannot be made free by their masters, they and their servitude a freedom to themselves, by serving them, not in deceitful fear but in faithful love, until iniquity be overpassed, and all man's power and principality disanulled, and God only be all in all.[29]

Here the gloomy deeply conservative aspect of Augustine's political philosophy makes itself apparent. We may have to put up with particular forms of subservience, such as that suffered by a colonized society, not because the colonized people have done wrong in themselves but because humankind as a whole has sinned. In terms of world society this is not a progressive view. Augustine's pessimism, sometimes reflected in the realist school, might pave the way for the acceptance of a highly unjust international order. Augustine seems in fact to expect little else.

To summarize Augustine's doctrine we might say that he is the point of origin of one distinctly Christian doctrine of the state and international society. The first precept of this doctrine is that the condition of humankind is one after the fall from grace. We are steeped in sin. Second, since we are all sinful and all our actions are conditioned by guilt this world is an alien world. Augustine turns away from the pagan worldly doctrines in present beneficence found in Greek philosophy to a seemingly joyless doctrine that implies, as a third precept, that there is no point in achieving any absolute good here on earth. Fourth, there is but one good and that good is God.

There are four other precepts that follow from these suppositions. The fifth precept is the one that provides Augustine's central teaching, namely that human society present and eternal is divided into two cities, the heavenly city and the earthly city. Sixth, a consequence of this view is that living Christians are always pilgrims in their present abode. Christians cannot be redeemed while they live. Yet, on the other hand, Christians cannot be sure that they will be saved in the afterlife and must seek to attain that state of grace by following God's will in their earthly lives. Seventh, the Church can provide some guidance for Christian pilgrims in pursuit of their goal, but membership of the Church is in itself no guarantee that the heavenly city will become our eternal abode. Eighth, all of this leaves the individual in a highly precarious position in relation to the worldly city. We have to respect the particular laws of our community, but not absolutely. We owe our allegiance first of all to God and only secondly to the earthly city. But we must not take our allegiance to the earthly city lightly: we should accept and foster the peace it offers. As temporal beings we are called upon to remain loyal to the earthly city while we remain within its confines.

Christian pessimism

While banishing for the present all prospect of human harmony and peace, the Christian tradition as represented by Augustine was at the same time seemingly responsible for erecting as a possibility the notion of a universal community beyond the problems and difficulties of existing society. According to this view, individuals are not only saving their souls by holding back from the fullest earthly life but also keeping open the possibility of bringing into being a perfectly harmonious community in the future.

This contrast between an imperfect present world and a perfect future world appears to have made its mark on the approach of theoreticians and politicians in the international arena. Those, like Niebuhr, of Augustine's pessimistic disposition have used the contrast to support decisions which have to be made to sustain the current political situation, arguing that nothing can be done immediately to make individuals and states better.

According to this view the conduct of international life is a matter of combatting evil with evil. War unavoidably arises in this situation. The evil perpetrated by the state in defending itself is not good in itself but it is seen as better than the spontaneous evil of the opponents of the state and the international order. Thus, as Holmes points out, there is only the slenderest justifications of war to be found in Augustine's writings.[30] What Augustine proposes is a relative rather than absolute theory of the just war.

The dichotomous Christian view of human life has, however, also led in the opposite direction. The recognition that this world is flawed and imperfect has led to the drive by some for the realization of a perfect 'one' world. The recognition of the equality of all individuals and groups by the Christian tradition has pressed forward this eschatological or millenialist trend. World-weary politicians who deal with the world as it is – with all its human failings (the Augustinian politician) – appear to bring into being their opposite: radical zealots who believe that the world can be ultimately freed of its imperfections. It may be that the one approach here is as unbalanced as the other.

Augustine has a fairly bleak Christian vision of the nature of human society. Humankind is divided into two: the vast majority are wicked beyond redemption, a small minority, however, have the ability to pass through this life to a greater beyond. It is on this chosen few that Augustine concentrates. The chosen few never know with certainty who they are. But those wishing to be among them on the Day of Judgement must disdain the pleasures, lusts and desires of this life and give their attention wholly to the *City of God.* Universal peace is truly other-worldly and only an elite from those presently existing may enjoy its fruits.

Politics and war are the spheres in which the wickedness of the human being is most apparent to all. States are entitled to use violence among themselves and against their citizens because no sort of order will prevail unless they do so. It is the duty of individuls to tolerate their present masters because no one can offer improvement from our present condition. For Augustine the fate of Greek society and the Roman Empire gave evidence of the folly of setting too much store by worldly events. Those civilizations were shaken from the outside by barbaric forces. The individual cannot seek salvation in human society nor in an earthly world community.

Augustine thinks that there can be progress towards peace, but this is a peculiar kind of peace. He takes it for granted that *Peace is the instinctive aim of all creatures, and is even the ultimate purpose of war.*[31] There is no person who does not wish for peace. Even wars, then, are waged with peace as their object. In fact, even when people wish a present state of peace to be disturbed they do so not because they hate peace, but because they desire the present peace to be exchanged for one that suits their wishes. Thus their desire is not that there should not be peace but that it should be the kind of peace they wish for. We see, then, that all human beings desire to be at peace with their own people, while wishing to impose their will upon those people's lives. For even when they wage war on others, their wish is to make those opponents their own people, if they can – to subject them, and to impose on them their own conditions of peace. Thus individuals and princes seek out all kinds of secular peace, but there can be nothing lasting about it.[32] For both the prince and the ordinary individual 'so long as he is in this mortal body, he is a pilgrim in a foreign land.' Genuine peace is internal and is to be gained through meditation and anticipation of the life beyond: 'The peace which is our special possession is ours in this life, as peace with God through faith; and it will be ours forever, a peace with God through open vision'.[33]

I find it difficult not to become impatient with this vision. It seems to me to provide too great an excuse for accepting present evils and doing little or nothing to overcome them. Reinhold Niebuhr takes a contrary view. Augustine's vision of a perfect community beyond the present world suggests to Niebuhr that the notion of community is preserved in face of the harshness of the world. Through this notion we are able to keep alive our love of humanity and it also provides a justification of those acts of morality we are able to see through.

But Augustine's doctrine is not one of progress. He does not accept that even the smallest concrete step forward towards a future world community can be taken or planned. Human life and consequently world society is caught in a continuous cycle of sin, forgiveness, shame, guilt and further sin. Some might regard this starkly realist doctrine as simply defeatist. Possibly there are grounds for greater optimism than Augustine was prepared to admit. It may be that human society does advance. Possibly Augustine was too caught up in the spirit of his own times, beset as they were by the problems of the decline and fall of the Roman Empire.

Notes

1. Cf. M.J. Smith (1986) *Realist Thought from Weber to Kissinger*, Baton Rouge, La: Lousiana State University Press, ch. 5.
2. R.M. Brown (ed.) (1986) *The Essential Reinhold Niebuhr*, New Haven, Conn: Yale University Press, p. 124.
3. *The Essential Niebuhr*, p. 124.
4. *The Essential Niebuhr*, p. 124.
5. M. Foster (1969) *Masters of Political Thought*, vol. 1, London: Harrap, p. 197.
6. *Masters of Political Thought*, p. 201.
7. *Masters of Political Thought*, p. 202.
8. *Masters of Political Thought*, p. 203.
9. *Masters of Political Thought*, p. 203.
10. *Masters of Political Thought*, p. 204.
11. *Masters of Political Thought*, p. 207; Augustine (1972) *City of God*, Harmondsworth: Penguin, p. 139.

12. *Masters of Political Thought*, p. 210; *City of God*, p. 866.
13. *Masters of Political Thought*, p. 213; *City of God*, p. 870.
14. *Masters of Political Thought*, p. 214; *City of God*, p. 873.
15. *Masters of Political Thought*, p. 216.
16. *Masters of Political Thought*, p. 216.
17. *Masters of Political Thought*, p. 217; *City of God*, p. 599.
18. *The Essential Niebuhr*, p. 127.
19. *City of God*, p. 861.
20. *City of God*, p. 861.
21. *City of God*, p. 861.
22. *City of God*, p. 861.
23. *City of God*, p. 861.
24. *City of God*, p. 861-2.
25. R.L. Holmes (1989) *On War and Morality*, Princeton, NJ: Princeton University Press, p. 128.
26. *Masters of Political Thought*, p. 217.
27. *Masters of Political Thought*, p. 219; *City of God*, p. 877.
28. *Masters of Political Thought*, p. 211; *City of God*, XIX, 15.
29. *Masters of Political Thought*, p. 211; *City of God*, XIX, 15.
30. *On War and Morality*, p. 128, p. 131-2.
    'If we cannot conform fully to God's law given our sinful nature, at least we can discern the traces of justice in our social life and within limits act accordingly. This provides the key to the possibility of just wars from a temporal or human perspective.... When a state has wronged another, either by failing to restore what it has unjustly taken or by refusing to punish wrongs committed by its citizens, one then has just cause to punish that state, providing the decision emanates from a legitimate authority'.
31. *City of God*, p. 866.
32. *City of God*, p. 873.
33. *City of God*, p. 892.

Further reading

Augustine (1972) *City of God*, Harmondsworth: Penguin.
Bathory, P.D. (1981) *Political Theory as Public Confession*, New Brunswick, NJ: Transaction Books.
Brown, P. (1979) *Augustine of Hippo: A Biography*, London: Faber.
Brown, R.M. (ed.) (1986) *The Essential Reinhold Niebuhr*, New Haven, Conn: Yale University Press.
Burleigh, J.H.S. (1950) *The City of God: A Study of St Augustine's Philosophy*, London: Westminster Press.
Chadwick, H. (1986) *Augustine*, Oxford: Oxford University Press.
Deane, H.A. (1963) *The Political and Social Ideas of St. Augustine*, New York: Columbia University Press.
Figgis, J.N. (1963) *The Political Aspects of St. Augustine's City of God*, Gloucester, Mass: Peter Smith.
PaoLucci, H. (1967) *The Political Writings of St. Augustine*, Chicago, Ill: Chicago University Press.

4 | AQUINAS: THE CATHOLIC VISION AND THE JUST WAR

Thomas Aquinas was born in 1224 or 1225, the son of a Neapolitian count, Landulph of Aquin. As a youth he studied in the Benedictine monastery of Monte Cassino and in 1239 he went on to study the liberal arts at the University of Naples. At Naples he first came into contact with the philosophy of Aristotle. In 1245 he went as a Dominican monk to study at the University of Paris and there he received instruction from the philosopher and theologian Albert the Great.[1] In 1256 Aquinas was himself admitted into the academic profession and taught in Paris until 1259. Between 1260 and 1270 he taught theology in his native Italy, partly in the papal court of Urban IV. He devoted his life to scholarship, producing an extraordinary number of works in his relatively short life, of which the most important is possibly the *Summa Theologiae*.

When Aquinas returned to Paris in 1268 he came into conflict with a rival theological and philosophical school, the Averroists, who sought to give a higher role to philosophy than religion. Aquinas emerged triumphant in this dispute managing to harmonize the insights of the revived philosophy of the pagan Greeks with the teachings of the Church. Aquinas is *the* philosopher of Roman Catholicism and his enormous contribution fully justified his elevation to sainthood. He was recalled to Italy in 1272 and died in 1274 while on a journey to Lyon. Foster quite rightly assesses him to be the greatest of the medieval scholastic philosophers.[2] Among his followers and admirers he became known as the 'angelic doctor'.

Aquinas's philosophy is a great work of synthesis. He seeks to construct the perfect system outside which nothing can fall. This synthesis is the Christian one of the infinite love of God and Aquinas includes within that love of all humankind, who are all God's creatures. A similar figure in the history of philosophy is Hegel who (as we shall see later) within his dialectical vision of *Geist* seeks to include all that is and has been. Aquinas shares the same ambition, trying at all times to subsume the individual within the whole. Aquinas's philosophy is testimony to the energy of a certain kind of human intellect which is never satisfied with incompleteness. But incompleteness and dissatisfaction within human experience there surely is.

In his short poem, *Pippa's Song,* which appears in the larger dramatic piece *Pippa Passes,* the Victorian poet Robert Browning ends with the words: 'God's in his heaven—/All's right with the world!'³ The optimism expressed in these words may be a reflection of Pippa's naivety or possibly a reflection of the English poet's attachment to romantic innocence. Whatever the words may reflect to Browning it seems that the sentiments are still with us. Many ordinary people and possibly some politicians look upon the world with an unquestioning contentment derived from religious faith. Aquinas is a philosophical representative of this unquestioning optimism. He recommends a faith in God which sees reason in the world (as it is) and on the whole advises our acceptance of things as they are.

Aquinas presents a natural view of world order. It is not simply the earthly world which is rationally structured: the whole of creation takes on this form. There is a spiritual world with God at its centre. From this world we get the right values for human life. Alongside this spiritual world is the temporal world where individuals seek to live according to the divine vision. Both together form a totality harmonized by God in his laws.

In this catholic vision spiritual and worldly authority and hierarchy are welcomed and accepted. But the rulers of states are not superior for its own sake. They are superior because they have a social function to perform. They perform that function on behalf of others. There is for Aquinas an element of duty in acting within a government. Just as citizens have a duty to obey legitimate governments so the members of such governments have a duty to act in accordance with law.

Aquinas finds no difficulty about the overlap between national and international society. We are subject to the same laws in both. Eternal law, divine law and natural law all extend beyond the boundaries of the state. Statesmen can discover therefore how to act in international society by consulting their reason. This use of reason will acquaint statesmen with the laws which govern international society. International law is then drawn from natural law, and diplomacy must also follow the recommendations of this law. Statesmen obey international law not simply because it is in their interests to do so but also because they are servants of the one God.

Divine and secular authority are in harmony with each other therefore because their ends are similar. The secular authorities are seeking obedience to the laws from their citizens and those laws derive their ultimate spiritual authority from God. In punishing those who disobey the laws of society the government for the most part reinforces divine law.

Aquinas's outlook leads to an almost cosily complacent conception of life. Everything is nearly as it ought to be. There is a prejudice in favour of our inherited social and international circumstances. States are living in harmony with each other because their leaders obey natural law which is straightforward enough for all to see. But what if natural law is difficult to discern in any particular situation? What if circumstances are so unique no law can be cited to regulate them? Aquinas does not account for the possibility that each state may interpret international law in its own way. Our reason may lead us in opposed directions, and not all want to act according to reason.

But even Aquinas's picture is not a wholly rosy one. He admits that it may be possible that one has an unjust ruler. Not all rulers are prepared to obey the commands of Gods or the demands of natural law. Here there are legitimate grounds for resistance. Equally some international conflict may have to be resolved by war. For this purpose there exists the just war doctrine.

We may legitimately oppose a tyrant. The reason why tyrannical government is unjust is 'because it is directed not to the common welfare but to the private benefit of the ruler'.[4] Aquinas does not see the overthrow of such a government as rebellion in the strict sense. He believes that the first belligerent act has been perpetrated by the ruler in acting in a dictatorial manner. Care has to be taken in mounting such opposition not to create more disorder than the public is already suffering.[5] Those leaders of the Baltic states who want to secede from the Soviet Union, since they regard the Union as an alien body imposed from the outside, might well heed Aquinas's advice and not press their opposition to Soviet institutions too hard. To reach a point where the disruption caused by rebellion is greater than the discontent already being experienced would, from Aquinas's viewpoint, be counter-productive. Aquinas thinks that where there is a conflict between tyrannical rulers and their people the blame for bloodshed lies more on the side of the bad ruler. It is the ruler who 'spreads discord and strife among the people subject to him, so hoping to control them more easily'.[6] It is not sedition to bring down such a ruler.

The just war

Aquinas takes it for granted that the harmony God proposed for the world is from time to time disrupted. War is an example of such disturbance of the natural order of things to be avoided unless circumstances dictate otherwise. And some circumstances may warrant a just war. There are three conditions under which a just war is possible. First, the authority of the ruler within whose competence it lies to declare war must be manifest; it is not possible for a private individual to declare war. Second, there has to exist a just cause. Those who are attacked for some offence must merit such treatment: an example of such an offence is where one state attacks another without warning and apparent cause. Third, for a war to be waged justly requires the right intention on the part of the belligerents. There must be an attempt to achieve some good object or an attempt to avoid some evil. Following Augustine the object of war must, however paradoxical it might seem, be peace. In Augustine's words 'the desire to hurt, the cruelty of vendetta, the stern and implacable spirit, arrogance in victory, the thirst for power, and all that is similar, all these are justly condemned in war.'[7]

The three conditions may, at first sight, appear to be insignificant. But their fulfilment or possible lack of fulfilment has played an important part in the shaping of policy in contemporary wars. Meeting the first condition caused untold difficulties for the United States in the course of the war against Vietnam. The proper authority of the President to prosecute the war was always under question from Congress and the American people. At no time did the American President seek the express approval of Congress for involvement through an official declaration of war.

It might be justifiably argued that the ability of the United States to wage the war was seriously undermined by this dispute about 'proper authority'. As Commander-in-Chief of United States Armed Forces the President had wide powers to act in defence of the national interest. But many in Congress argued that full constitutional authority for the conflict could be gained only through the express support of Congress. Matters came to a head in 1973 when Congress passed the War Powers Resolution which forbade the President from committing troops to hostilities except after a declaration of war or other express authority from Congress.[8] Consequently it may have come as a considerable relief to President Bush when Congress in 1991 voted by a small majority for the use of force against Saddam Hussein during the invasion of Iraq.

The second condition seems equally as difficult to fulfil. Here there is possible a great vagueness as to what might constitute a proper cause. What are to be counted as wrongs among states? Can the manner in which states treat their own citizens be regarded as a just cause for invasion by another state? Some commentators regard the intervention by the United States within Latin American countries to suppress apparently authoritarian regimes as perfectly justifiable. Equally Brezhnev enunciated his own doctrine with regard to eastern Europe which permitted intervention in brother socialist states. Aquinas appears to offer no direct grounds for intervening in this way. States are authorized to declare war seemingly only on grounds of self-defence. Conceivably this might lead to intervention where the actions of a neighbouring state were apparently so de-stabilizing that they effected the security of one's own state. But no elaborate theory of intervention may be drawn from Aquinas's notion of wrong or just cause since he takes it for granted that wars will be fought against 'external enemies'.[9] The implication is that opponents need already to have taken up arms against you in order to warrant your intervention.

The third condition is perhaps the most interesting of the three. This requires the right intention on the part of those who prosecute a war. And the right intention should not be war itself: the object of a just war has to be peace. Aquinas quotes approvingly Augustine's remark that 'for the true followers of God even wars are peaceful, not being made for greed or out of cruelty, but from desire of peace, to restrain the evil and assist the good.'[10] But it is extremely difficult to know whether or not this condition is being adhered to. Does the condition imply that a military commander should show no enthusiasm for war? We may be expecting too much of professional soldiers not to want them to look positively on their trade. States expect armed forces to kill on their behalf, members of the armed forces may well expect in return some respect and positive support for their work. It may not be right to glory in war but it may none the less have beneficial effects.

An interesting development of Aquinas's just war theory is that of Paul Ramsey and others who suggest a doctrine of 'double-effect' may be deduced from Aquinas's thinking.[11] Aquinas argues it is legitimate to act in self-defence providing the action taken is in proportion to the wrong perpetrated. Thus if someone threatens to kill you by raising a knife to you, you may well be justified in doing harm to them, providing the harm is limited to what is necessary to repel the attack. The purpose from beginning to end is one's own defence. The defender's act of aggression is the outcome of this intent, not its object. As an extension of this, interpreters of Aquinas have argued 'civilian or noncombatant casualities may be "permitted" in war, but only as an unintended, unavoidable, indirect effect that does not exceed of the intended good effect against a legitimate military target.'[12] Thus even this argument of double-effect is not a warrant to kill indiscriminately in defence of one's nation. The good intention of defence may become bad if the destruction brought about is wholly out of proportion to the wrong caused.

This issue came to the fore in the conflict between Iraq and the coalition led by the United States over the occupation of Kuwait. In his speeches President Bush tried to demonstrate that the war with Iraq was just on the grounds of Iraq's failure to make good its initial aggression by withdrawing from Kuwait. Bush argued that the United States would do everything to avoid the slaughter of the innocent by directing its campaign solely at military targets. The United States' leader sought to take the higher moral ground by arguing along these lines, pointing in contrast to the Iraqi leader's apparent indifference to the cost in human lives of the war. But there is a drawback in appealing to the just war doctrine, particularly its proportionality aspect. The drawback is that some may argue that there is no rationale for a war at all where the cost in human lives looks likely to be incalculable. Some Catholic writers have argued this in relation to the Iraqi conflict. The dangers which arise from the possible use of chemical and nuclear weapons available to the combatants outweigh any possible advantages pursuing the war may have.[13] Thus Aquinas's political standpoint might likely recommend itself to political leaders who are in charge of already dominant states. Browning's joyous phrase from *Pippa's Song* might therefore adequately represent the standpoint of the Victorian ruling class in charge of a successful Empire, and that of any subsequent successful world power. The leaders of a minor, possibly subjugated state might not take so readily to the doctrine which favoured so obviously the established order. Finding the international order not to their liking the leaders of a minor state might believe that reason was inadequately reflected in the world and they were entirely justified in seeking to amend it. None the less, even they (as leaders of a small state) might advocate Aquinas's doctrine of acceptance to their subjects. The leaders might feel that God had got it about right in relation to their subordinate position of their own subjects! I find this aspect of Aquinas's outlook somewhat too complacent to be appealing.

Nature and law

Aquinas's optimism is derived by combining the philosophy of Aristotle with the doctrines of the founders of the Christian Church. Aristotle regarded each object or condition as performing a function which accorded with nature. There was a sense to things as they stood. The politics of the city and the relations among city-states reflected a functioning order. This harmonious view of the universe Aquinas combines with the Christian account of the drama and tragedy of individual life. For Aquinas the drama and tragedy of individual life is compensated for by the order of the whole. As Sabine and Thorson put it, for Aquinas,

> the universe forms a hierarchy reducing from God at its summit down to the lowest being. Every being acts under the internal urge of its own nature, seeking the good or form of perfection natural to its bent, and finding its place in the ascending order according to its degree of perfection.[14]

Whereas Augustine appears to favour the idea of two radically separate worlds – the secular world of wickedness and vice and the divine truly humane world of the City of God – Aquinas tries to bring the two together (through the agency of Aristotle's philosophy). Following Aristotle, Aquinas sees the secular world as fulfilling important purposes of its own. These purposes such as work and procreation he regards as implementing God's will. Secular life need not represent a pilgrimage in an alien land; it can be rewarding in its own terms. For Aquinas the divine world is not wholly the opposite (or the other) of the world of humans, by transcending the secular world it compliments it. Augustine may have reflected the radicalism of the Church founders in his apparent rejection of the attractions of earthly life. In contrast, Aquinas might be seen as reflecting the position of the Christian faith as an established religion. Now accepted (or embraced) by earthly powers the Christian can afford to look more generously upon the established order.

Aquinas does look more tolerantly upon the world than Augustine. Worldly authority functions for Aquinas not merely to carry out worldly purposes. The ruler as well as being an agent of human society is also an agent of God:

> Just as the divine control is exercised over all created bodies and over all spiritual powers, so does the control of reason extend over the members of the body and the other faculties of the soul: so, in a certain sense, reason is to man what God is to the universe.[15]

With Augustine, human life, particularly international society, seems beyond the control of reason. The chaos and injustice of the world appears to reflect man's propensity to sin. But Aquinas sees less chaos and sin: with him nature and human nature are not the other of God.

In using their reason to govern, rulers are reflecting God's will. Following Plato and Aristotle, Aquinas sees the just human being as one who employs reason to subordinate desires and needs to a greater purpose. By analogy rulers are perfectly justified in using their power to subordinate the various parts of the community to the requirements of the whole. If rulers think about their role in this light they will become 'fired with a good for justice'[16] because they will see themselves as administering justice 'in the name of God'.

This may appear to be an improvement upon Augustine's indifference to earthly authority. Aquinas does at least see government as fulfilling a useful ethical purpose. Conflict among states is a disruption for Aquinas and not simply to be expected as with Augustine. However, there may be dangers attached to seeing the ruler as the earthly representative of a divine power. Aquinas assumes that reason will dictate in an unambiguous way the measures a ruler should adopt and thus the authority of the ruler will be wholly justified. However, the reasoning of no two people seems to be entirely the same. What one person sees as reasonable, another may see as entirely unreasonable. Justice is not as easily attained as Aquinas suggests.

Aquinas founds his view of political conduct upon authority. Statesmen act not to please themselves or solely to serve the needs of their state: they act on behalf of God. What they decide therefore has upon it the hallmark of the divine will. For Aquinas there has to be *Majesty* in the state. Moreover, this authority takes on the mark of paternal authority since *God is the Father*. The consoling aspect of Aquinas's optimistic (where for the most part things are as they ought to be) view of political conduct has (in my opinion) a great deal to do with this patriarchal basis; this patriarchal authority is spelled out in a fourfold system of laws:

1 *Eternal law*   which is reason in the mind of God according to which the whole universe is governed.
2 *Natural law*   which is reason's participation in the eternal law.
3 *Human law*   which is to be found in laws devised by human beings in particular societies.
4 *Divine law*   which is the law given to humankind through revelation of which the supreme example is Moses's receiving the Ten Commandments on Mount Sinai.[17]

Eternal law has no beginning in time and no end in time. It both pre-exists the universe and exists simultaneously with it. Eternal law is the work of God or is, rather, his essence. Everything that is, obeys these eternal laws in one form or another. Thus the laws discovered by natural science are themselves part of God's plan. Nothing can penetrate the complete world of eternal law: it is a self-justifying totality. However, human beings are related to eternal law in a different way from the manner in which inanimate nature is related to it. Humans are capable of comprehending and acting upon God's commands.

Eternal law and natural law are intimately connected. Natural law is the name for the aspects of eternal law that are open to human comprehension. Aquinas takes the view that certain rules of human experience and conduct are intuitively known to us all. They underlie our normal relations with other individuals and states. This kind of knowledge is not open to controversy. We can be fairly sure as to what course of action natural law dictates. In international relations it forms the basis for international law. Possibly this is where the crusading spirit derives from in Christian conduct. Catholic Christians can be convinced of their own adherence to natural law and consequently of others who fail to respect it. There is an aspect of Aquinas that is not interested in conjecture, opinion nor unresolved disputes. He has to have one answer. But so many philosophers have taken this view of life and have ended up at odds with each other on this account. Although everyone of this disposition claims certainty and truth, what we in fact have is a variety of certainties and truths. If anyone of these certainties is pushed too far intolerance results. As O'Connor puts it, as opposed to Aquinas's view of knowledge as 'intuitive, certain and incorrigible' it is difficult not to find persuasive a 'view of knowledge which is tentative, experimental and corrigible'.[18]

To be weighed against the apparent dogmatism of Aquinas's account of natural law is his more flexible approach to human law. Human law is 'devised by man, for the particular and detailed regulation of what the natural law ordains'.[19] Like divine law, human law is positive requiring legislation and enforcement to exist. Aquinas thinks there is a natural disposition to good in human individuals but this is not uniformly experienced. Some have to be restrained from wrongdoing by force. Thus states enact laws which reflect their practice and customs. Human laws may therefore vary in their stipulations from society to society and are also subject to change. They are subject to change on two grounds. First, because human reason is fallible and may err in its interpretation of what constitutes a wrongful act. Second, human laws may change because circumstances change. But human law is subordinate to natural law and should not knowingly depart from it. Although human law is mutable it is not arbitrary.

Whereas Augustine argues for the separateness of secular and religious authority Aquinas puts forward the more bracing doctrine that the authority of state rulers is ultimately subordinate to the Church. This has interesting implications for international relations. A Catholic of Aquinas's disposition might regard rulers as holding authority in God's name and therefore being subject to eternal and natural law. Thus rulers who did not regard themselves as subject to the constraints of Christian beliefs would represent an anomaly from the Catholic standpoint, an anomaly the Catholic might expect to be overcome in the fullness of time. Thus, for instance, just wars are not fought in vain. They may bring immoral leaders and states round to Christian ways.

Aquinas argues that religious authority is superior because 'the end of temporal felicity is subordinate to that of eternal blessedness, which alone is an end in itself'.[20] Thus for the Catholic the Pope is justifiably the head of the temporal human enterprise, standing above all politicians. The secular leader is concerned solely with the behaviour of individuals now, whereas the state is concerned with their higher perfection. 'For those into whose charge the care of subordinate ends has been committed ought to be subject to him whose charge is the supreme end, and to be directed by his authority.'[21] Aquinas compares the ruler's task with that of the ship's carpenter whose job it is to keep the ship in good repair. The task of the Church is like that of the pilot which is to steer the ship successfully to port. The Church then has a legitimate interest in the whole of humankind and secular rulers ought to accept and respect this interest. Aquinas's recipe for world harmony is quite clearly the subordination of political rulers to the higher ends of the Church. Although not everyone's view, this position is not without its contemporary advocates.

Notes

1. M. Grabmann (1928) *Thomas Aquinas*, London: Longman, pp. 2–3.
2. M. Foster (1969) *Masters of Political Thought*, vol. 1, London: Harrap, p. 239.
3. H. Milford (ed.) (1972) *Poems of Robert Browning*, Oxford: Oxford University Press, p. 19.
4. Aquinas (1965) *Selected Political Writings*, Oxford: Basil, Blackwell, p. 161.
5. *Selected Political Writings*, p. 161.

6. *Selected Political Writings,* p. 161.
7. *Selected Political Writings,* p. 161.
8. M.J.C. Vile (1983) *Politics in the USA,* London: Hutchinson, p. 164.
9. *Selected Political Writings,* p. 159.
10. *Selected Political Writings,* pp. 159–61.
11. D.L. Davidson (1983) *Nuclear Weapons and the American Churches,* Boulder, Col: Westview Press, p. 7.
12. *Nuclear Weapons and the American Churches,* p. 7.
13. 'A just conflict, or just a conflict?', *Time,* 11 February 1991: 36–7.
14. G.H. Sabine and T.L. Thorson (1973) *A History of Political Thought,* Hinsdale, Ill: Holt-Saunders, p. 237.
15. *Selected Political Writings,* p. 67.
16. *Selected Political Writings,* p. 67.
17. *Selected Political Writings,* pp. 113–30.
18. D.J. O'Connor (1967) *Aquinas and Natural Law,* London: Macmillan, p. 84.
19. *Masters of Political Thought,* p. 250.
20. *Masters of Political Thought,* p. 259.
21. *Masters of Political Thought,* p. 262.

Further reading

Aquinas (1965) *Selected Political Writings,* Oxford: Basil Blackwell.
Aquinas (1967) *Selected Writings,* London: Dent.
Coplestone, F.C. (1955) *Aquinas,* Harmondsworth: Penguin.
D'Entreves, A.P. (1959) *The Medieval Contribution to Political Thought,* New York: Humanities Press.
Kenny, A. (1980) *Aquinas,* Oxford: Oxford University Press.
O'Connor, D.J. (1967) *Aquinas and Natural Law,* London: Macmillan.
Ramsey, P. (1961) *War and the Christian Conscience,* Durham, North Caroline: Duke University Press.
Russell, F.H. (1975) *The Just War in the Middle Ages,* Cambridge: Cambridge University Press.
Tranoy, K. (1964) 'Aquinas', in D.J. O'Connor (ed.) *A Critical History of Western Philosophy,* New York: Macmillan.
Weiskeipl, J.A. (1975) *Friar T.D. Aquino,* Oxford: Basil Blackwell.

5 | MACHIAVELLI: REALPOLITIK

As with Plato an account of Machiavelli's life goes some way towards explaining his political philosophy. Machiavelli was born in 1469 in Florence, one of a large number of small independent Italian states which had enjoyed a republican tradition based on trade and commerce. But Italian politics was at that time, as is often so nowadays as well, in a condition of great turmoil. Italy had been invaded by the French in 1494,[1] the French armies reaching as far south as Naples. The French vied with the Spanish for influence over the Italian peninsula. In the circumstances, the Florentine republic was in a state of disarray. The *Medici* family was a continually powerful force in Florentine politics, but the French invasion precipitated change which led to the last period of republican rule, in which Machiavelli was to play a prominent part.

From 1494 to 1498 Florence was ruled by the priest *Savonarola*, a somewhat shadowy figure said to have powers of prophecy; it was his domination of the Medici family which brought him to prominence. However, he was as rapidly discarded by the Florentine populace as he had been taken up. The demise of Savonarola was much to Machiavelli's advantage, however: in 1498, at the age of 29, he was made secretary to the Second Chancery, a position of considerable influence. Machiavelli's influence over Florentine politics was at its height from 1502 to 1512 while his friend Piero *Soderini* was head of state.

There is no doubt that this period of government was quite crucial to the development of Machiavelli's thinking. While head of the Second Chancery, Machiavelli undertook missions to the French Court (of Louis XII) and to that of Emperor Maximilian. He also experienced some of *Cesare Borgia*'s campaigning in Romagna. Borgia was an immensely colourful figure who may well have represented something of a model for the portrait of the successful *Prince*. In addition Machiavelli was an observer at the papal election of 1503 of Julius II. Machiavelli also played a considerable part in the reorganization of the Florentine army from 1507 onwards – an experience on which he was heavily to draw in writing his most well-known work, *The Prince*.

Machiavelli's fortunes took a turn for the worse as the influences of the Medici family once again grew in Italy. This was fired by the success of the Spanish in defeating the French at Ravenna in 1509. The Spanish armies invaded Italy in 1512 to remove the French, and it was as a consequence of their success that the Florentine republic fell. Soderini had followed a consistently pro-French policy.

It can be truly said that Machiavelli experienced at first hand politics and the relations among states. The period 1512–13 saw the point of the lowest ebb of Machiavelli's career. He was suspected by the Medicis of having played a part in an attempt to overthrow the new government. He was imprisoned and tortured, but it was this cruel twist of fortune which was to lead to Machiavelli's greatest contribution to history. On being released from prison Machiavelli made use of his enforced retirement to write *The Prince* (1514), which is a treatise on politics and history from a practical point of view, and his *Discourses on Livy*, an appreciation and criticism of an account of the Roman Empire given by a famous Roman historian.

Machiavelli did not see *The Prince* simply as an academic work. It was, he hoped, to provide him with the path back to political power. He dedicated his book to Lorenzo de Medici, the new ruler of Florence, and presented him with a copy. *The Prince* was intended to demonstrate both Machiavelli's dedication to the Florentine state and his usefulness to a *new Prince*. Machiavelli saw his commitment as being to the Florentine state rather than the previous regime which he had served. In *The Prince* Machiavelli conceives his role as that of political theorist and adviser. This was a model a number of later political thinkers were to follow, and one that has been extremely influential in the development of international relations as a subject. Many distinguished American writers in the field, such as Hans Morgenthau and Henry Kissinger, also played extremely important roles in advising and acting on behalf (in Kissinger's case) of American governments.

However, Machiavelli was not successful in his attempts to get back to power. But his literary talents were recognized by his peers, and he was given a commission to write a *History of Florence* which he completed in 1525, two years before his death. In his life Machiavelli was a diplomat, statesman and scholar. He brought all the combined wisdom of his three careers to bear upon his writing of *The Prince* and *Discourses*.

Machiavelli's conception of politics

To understand the novelty of Machiavelli's approach to politics we must recall some of the main features of the ancient and medieval tradition of political thought which form the background to his own thinking. First, ancient political thought was heavily ethical in tone. Plato and Aristotle were greatly concerned with questions of what constituted good citizenship. In contrast medieval political thought was heavily dominated by religious issues. Aquinas, following Augustine, gave a great deal of attention to the question of God's authority in temporal life. Aquinas tells us in what ways he thinks rulers are circumscribed in their actions by religious belief. Machiavelli departs radically from such preoccupations. He is more concerned with what people actually do than what they ought to do. Machiavelli sets out not from the ideal, but rather from the behaviour he sees before him in everyday life and politics. Some commentators therefore see him as a realist political thinker. As Warren Winiarski says in the *History of Political Philosophy*, Machiavelli 'effected a revolution from the dominion of Plato and Aristotle, who had taught man what they ought to do. Machiavelli teaches what men *do*'.[2] The emphasis in Artistole and Plato is on politics helping to achieve the good life for the citizen morally defined, whereas the emphasis with Machiavelli is on how to gain and retain political power.

The Christian tradition represented by Aquinas and Augustine stressed God's presence in the world; that earthly life followed a course which reflected God's will. Generally speaking Christian writers present a political theory of acceptance and resignation before earthly powers. The Christian stress on the possibility of the eternal salvation of the human soul takes attention away from present right and wrong. Misfortune and injustice in this life may be compensated for in a later everlasting life. So the worldly ends pursued by political leaders are not of crucial interest to the Christian. Christians focus on the world community of God to which all, regardless of race or nation, may aspire.

Machiavelli breaks with the ethical and religious views of politics. Instead of seeing politics from the standpoint of Christian individual or the good citizen, he views it from the standpoint of the ruler, the state and the nation. Instead of politics being a matter of trying to determine and follow values which reflect a higher ethos, it becomes a technical matter of how best to hold on to power. Thus instead of the considered treatise for the intelligent and responsible citizen Machiavelli gives us a handbook for princes.

But Machiavelli does not put his talents at the disposal of the ruler in a thoroughly mercenary way. His insights are not simply made available to the highest bidder. There is a civic pride in the politics which Machiavelli offers. He regards his services as valuable because they are directed towards the survival and well-being of his state. He disdains flattery and lies, he offers his advice in a dispassionate truthful way. He stands back from political life and tries to see it as it truly is. As he says in a touching letter to Lorenzo de Medici,

> I have not found among my belongings anything as dear to me or that I value as much as my understanding of the deeds of great men, won by me from a long acquaintance with contemporary affairs and a continuous study of the ancient world?'[3]

Here we find the beginnings of modern political science both in its possibly beneficial sense of seeking an objective understanding of human society, and in its more controversial sense of offering suggestions to rulers as to how they might govern more successfully. It is within this culture that the study of international relations, as typified in the career of Henry Kissinger, who moved from being a Harvard professor to being secretary of state, has grown. Also a key school of thought in international relations has been that of power politics. Interesting representatives of this school are Georg Schwarzenberger and Hans Morgenthau. This school takes its point of departure from Machiavelli.

What then are the most important precepts of Machiavelli's view of politics? In Machiavelli's opinion,

> the main foundations of every state, . . . are good laws and good arms; and because you cannot have good laws without good arms, and where there are good ones, good laws inevitably follow, I shall not discuss laws but give my attention to arms.[4]

Everything takes second place to the power of the state and the success of its rulers, Machiavelli's experience tells him that this has ultimately to be based upon *force*. Because of his decision to put political power before all else, and his apparent contempt for conventional morality Machiavelli's name became synonymous with that of the devil: ('Old Nick'). But it is not true that Machiavelli seeks to overthrow all morality in *The Prince*, rather he is proposing a *new morality* which places success in the pursuit of political power before all else. There is a civic virtue in the pursuit of power that Machiavelli sets forward. The Prince is committed to establishing his power as a prerequisite for the success of his state. All citizens gain from the success and prestige of their state.

In section 18 of *The Prince*, where Machiavelli deals with the question 'How Princes should honour their word', he says: 'In the actions of all men, and especially of princes, where there is no court of appeal, *one judges by the result.*'[5] Where princes use the arms under their control to ensure their authority within and without the state they will be judged right because *'the common people are always impressed by appearances and results'*.[6] In general, it was wise for the Prince to maintain good faith and not deceive those with whom he deals. However, in Machiavelli's view, if it will enhance his power and the power of the state, then it is correct to act in defiance of good faith. It is most important that the Prince *appear* to be honest and to act in good faith, but it is better than he should not always practise these qualities. To the innocent onlooker these suggestions seem to be highly immoral, but for Machiavelli the logic of politics makes them necessary.

Machiavelli makes a similar point when he discusses the politics of Ferdinand of Aragon, with Isabella of Castile, ruler of Spain. In Machiavelli's time Ferdinand succeeded in adding Naples to the territory ruled by the Spanish crown, and brought the whole of Spain under his control. Machiavelli says of him,

> A certain contemporary ruler, whom it is better not to name, never preaches anything except peace and good faith, and he is an enemy of both one and the other, and if he had ever honoured either of them he would have lost either his standing or his state many times over.[7]

Contemporary experience shows that princes who have achieved great things have been those who have given their word lightly, who have known how to trick people with their cunning.

Machiavelli's view of history: 'Virtue' and 'Fortune'

What is Machiavelli's justification for advocating this amoral course of action? Machiavelli has a very low view of human nature. Princes need not be honest and keep their word because 'men are wretched creatures who would not keep their word to you'. People are, in general, 'ungrateful fickle, liars, and deceivers, they shun danger and are greedy for profit'.[8] They are your friends while things go well for you, but should you suffer a reverse they shun you like the plague.

This leads Machiavelli to consider how rulers should treat those who are citizens under them. Because humans are untrustworthy and fickle, treating them well will not be enough to ensure their loyalty. If rulers have to choose between being loved or feared it is far better for rulers to choose to be feared because then there will be less chance of being disobeyed and having their will resisted.

> *The bond of love is one which men, wretched creatures that they are, break when it is to their advantage to do so; but fear is strengthened by a dread of punishment which is always effective.*[9]

Although the Prince should do the best he can to be respected and loved he should not worry himself *unduly should he gain a reputation for cruelty.* Should his cruelty, properly exercised, succeed in maintaining his rule it will have more than served its purpose.[10]

Machiavelli would meet the reproach that his *Prince* is immoral with the answer that a ruler cannot afford to be otherwise. In a world of beasts rulers cannot survive unless they act like a beast (with the cunning of a fox and the daring and force of the lion). 'The fact is that a man who wants to act virtuously in every way necessarily comes to grief among so many who are not virtuous'.[11] A Prince cannot neglect how people actually act in a pursuit of an ideal as to how people ought to act. If your opponent acts unfairly, you put yourself at unnecessary disadvantage when you yourself seek always to act fairly. Thus Machiavelli does not see it as the task of political leaders to set public standards, rather they should work within the standards and, where necessary, break the standards already being employed.

Machiavelli's view of history: 'Virtue' and 'Fortune'

Machiavelli was a great student of history. He wrote the lengthy *Discourses on Livy* at the same time as *The Prince*. Machiavelli believed that history held lessons from which any successful ruler should seek to learn. Human beings progress by imitation: if they tread where others have trodden before, they will do so with greater confidence. We cannot entirely create our own lives and our history in the way we wish. Confidence in action flows from a repetition of what others have done with elements of innovation.

So history is not an open book in which people and their leaders can write whatever they like. It is governed to a large extent by *Fortune*. However, Machiavelli is not one of those who believes that it is entirely governed by fortune. He sees a hand for the free will of humans to play in the progress of events. The course of events can be modified by the prudence of people

> because free choice cannot be ruled out, I believe that it is probably true that fortune is the arbiter of half the things we do, leaving the other half or so to be controlled by ourselves.[12]

At times the course of events dictated by fortune becomes a torrent which people cannot resist. However, at other quieter times, precautions can be taken, preparations and places can be made for the next great flood (of events). This is where the virtue of rulers and the wisdom of Princes come in. Great leaders correctly anticipate the path of events, intervene to set things on their way, and turn events to their advantage and that of their citizens. Impetuosity and audacity play their part here,

> *because fortune is a woman and if she is to be submissive it is necessary to beat and coerce her. Experience shows that she is more often subdued by men who do this than by those who act coldly. Always, being a woman, she favours young men,* because they are less circumspect and more ardent, and because they command her with greater audacity.[13]

We might remark that this is a partial and impetuous comment by Machiavelli himself. He presents a view of political wisdom which is the contrary of Aristotle's. Aristotle sees practical wisdom coming with age and regards the spontaneity and impetuosity of youth as something to be feared. Machia-

velli's approach seems to carry the greater risk. We may envisage circumstances where an act of daring might produce great political dividends, but
as likely as not bold moves can lead to downright failure. For example, it was
a bold move of the Russian leader Gorbachev to allow eastern Europe to step
out of the grip of centralist communism. But only time will tell whether the
move will be successful. In the meanwhile the internal Soviet consequences
of the change appear not to be too positive for President Gorbachev.
Machiavelli's argument for his audacious approach is that there is so little
certainty in social and political life that to adhere to Aristotle's conservative
politics may well court disaster. Policies have to be modified to accord with
circumstances to be successful, sometimes drastically so.

Machiavelli's dilemma

Machiavelli's Prince must tread a difficult path between immorality and
justice. Both to act, and to appear to act, justly can be of considerably benefit
to a ruler. Rules cannot be held in complete contempt and hatred by their
subjects: to be held in contempt will ultimately lead to their downfall.
Machiavelli suggests that the Prince's best means of avoiding the hatred of
citizens is not to be 'rapacious and aggressive with regard to the property
and women of his subjects'.[14] The citizens will forgive him dealing harshly
and unscrupulously with his political opponents if he succeeds in establishing his rule; however, they will not forgive him if he abuses his power to
deprive them of *their rights*. The Prince has to combine harshness and
injustice towards his opponents with compassion and justice towards his
best citizens.

Machiavelli's advice seems on the whole very sound. But can a Prince
maintain his power by relying on double standards in morality and the force
of arms? Machiavelli's *Prince* is told to trust no one, but to take advantage of
the truth of others. He is told to respect no individual's rights, but he accepts
others' respect of his rights. He is told to use force to establish justice (and
cruelty if needs be) but he depends on others putting justice before force and
abstaining from cruelty. I conclude that Machiavelli's advice to a Prince
succeeds only where others accept moral standards the Prince rejects,
where others are content to be ruled and accept that their ruler is above
ordinary morality and justice. This is a precarious balance indeed. It can be
upset easily where the Princes opponents take on the same system of values
as the Prince himself.

Machiavelli's aspirations for himself and for his country became apparent
here in his approach to the situation of Italy and its many city-states. In the
past the prospects for unification had seemed poor. Clearly Machiavelli felt
very deeply the domination of Italy by foreign powers such as Spain and
France. But now: 'I believe that so many things conspire to favour a new
Prince, that I cannot imagine there ever was a time more suitable than the

present'.¹⁵ Machiavelli cites the examples of Moses emerging under the Egyptian rule of the Israelites, and Cyrus and the Persians. Cesare Borgia at one time looked a possible contender for the rule, but he overreached himself. Machiavelli now looks to Lorenzo de Medici – his own new Prince in Florence – to lead Italy to its salvation. God has obviously prepared the way partly for Lorenzo: now it is his turn to take up the challenge.

The key to the success of Lorenzo's campaign is the raising of a citizen's army. These are the most loyal troops. They are able to identify with that for which they fight, so they will be the match of any mercenary army. Where men fight for money alone they are not to be depended on. If Lorenzo improves the infantry and the cavalry the Florentine army will frighten the Spaniards and the Swiss. Machiavelli quotes Livy in support of the demand for a war against Italy's aggressors. 'Because a necessary war is a just war and where there is hope only in arms, those arms are holy.'¹⁶

Machiavelli's political theory appears to bring us properly on to the scene of international politics. He seems to have no great concern for the role of citizens in the state, the theme that greatly occupied the Greeks and the early Christian thinkers. Machiavelli seems only to speak of citizens to the extent that they can strengthen or weaken a state. He seems most at home in talking of wars, alliances, glory, cruelty, the course of history and *princes*.

Although clearly aware of the dangers of political life Machiavelli writes as though there is enjoyment to be gained from engaging in diplomacy and interstate affairs. Machiavelli depicts the drama of political life and gives would-be statesmen some guidance as to how they might survive in the cut and thrust of relations among states.

Machiavelli's main object of concern appears to be the conduct of political life. The *Prince* begins with a discussion about how principalities (or states) are acquired by their leaders. He seems not to be greatly concerned with the historical facts at issue but rather sees the facts as a guide to how a principality might be most successfully ruled. What comes across is the practical statesman's approach. Political life is not seemingly seen solely as an object of study but also as a series of obstacles to be successfully negotiated. As we have seen, Aristotle placed great stress on experience, but for Machiavelli there are equally important factors, such as daring and audacity. Quickness of mind, a rapid ability to calculate advantages and disadvantages and a necessary physical fitness weigh the scales more in favour of the young.

Machiavelli appears to think that it is best to see political life as governed by dispositions rather than rules. Nothing in political life is wholly predictable. Allies can become opponents, friends can become enemies, enemies friends and opponents allies. Fortune plays its part. Machiavelli generously estimates that about half the events in history are brought about through what he calls *virtue* (the role of individual leaders) and half are brought about by *fortune*. Thus, the spin off of the wheel of fortune is not without its opportunities for the enterprising individual. Calculating properly the disposition of forces the leader may turn events to his advantage.

In this kaleidoscopic world of vying interests and powers there are some guidelines Machiavelli suggests may be laid down. First, it does not pay to take too high a view of human nature. 'Men are obstinate in their ways, men prosper so long as fortune and policy are in accord, and when there is a clash they fail'.[17] What is more, 'Men are so simple, and so much creatures of circumstances, that the deceiver will always find someone ready to be deceived'. This conclusion is reinforced in the *Discourses*,[18] where he says 'men never do good unless necessity drives them to it; but when they are free to choose and can do just as they please, confusion and disorder become everywhere rampant'.[19]

Second, it is results that count. Machiavelli estimates that nothing is more successful than success. What is first of all judged to be a risky enterprise will be subsequently regarded as a superb manoeuvre if it turns out to be successful. Means have to be adjusted to ends and ends to means in political life. A good end may justify the use of foul means providing those means are successful. But it may pay also to abandon a good end if there are no successful means of achieving it. Thus ends have to be adjusted to the means available. Most of our knowledge of the world we derive through our sight. Where we see the appearances of good fortune, wealth, beauty and prosperity we shall judge (on the whole) that individuals are acting well. Politicians who (maybe following Augustine) turn their back on worldly values to attain higher goals make an error.

Third, be prepared to break your promises: or give your word lightly. Partly this approach is justified because this is how others may act towards you. Partly the approach is justified because it may bring results. The two assumptions, of course, conflict. The second relies on the gullibility of individuals and the first suggests they are not. But life is diverse. People are different and in different moods people are more gullible than other times. Where morality and political expediency conflict, Machiavelli suggests that the prince might follow the path of expediency.

Fourth, be cruel when this is necessary to achieve your goals. Politicians ought not to aim at being cruel for its own sake but where it can bring dividends then it is advisable for them to act accordingly. The saturation bombing of Dresden may now appear to many as a deplorable act; however, it may have been calculated at the time that the effect on German civilian morale was sufficient to justify it. Machiavelli is not averse to a prince gaining a reputation for cruelty. The restraints imposed by morality on individuals cannot be readily observed, but fear can be detected more easily.

Fifth, prudent leaders direct their policy internally towards the majority. If they can keep the majority happy, they can deal fairly readily with the problems created by the minority. To satisfy the majority the prince clearly has to avoid the hatred of the masses.[20]

Sixth, policy has to be varied according to the circumstances. There is no combination of forces that will always succeed. Aristotle in recommending practical wisdom may be successful most of the time but where enterprise and risk are necessary his approach may well fail.[21] Not even experience can always guarantee success. Thus the prince must show the utmost flexibility in pursuing his purposes.

Seventh, a prince may seek advice but should be careful about accepting it: 'good advice, whomever it comes from, depends on the shrewdness of the person who seeks it, and not the shrewdness of the prince on good advice'.[22] Those who give advice should think more of their prince than themselves; those who appear to put themselves first are not to be trusted.

There is great value in these seven suggestions. A prudent leader would doubtlessly examine them quite closely. Political life may tend in the direction Machiavelli suggests if his account of the nature of human society is at all correct. Yet there is a final difficulty with his approach. Machiavelli's ethics of power may lead the politician into a quagmire of relativity. Since following this ethos, leaders have always to temper their ends to suit their means the goal may not seem worth pursuing. The politics and diplomacy of a state may become aimless as pressures mount. The state that looks solely to power may lose any sense of purpose in its existence. Power is (in my opinion) desirable because it is a means to other ends such as wealth and security. Where power itself becomes the objective then its attainment becomes empty. Thus to make it at all attractive even Machiavellian politics should fit in the framework of a larger purpose. In international politics the pursuit of power without regard to ethical concerns is possibly a recipe for disaster.

Notes

1. Q. Skinner (1978) *The Foundations of Modern Political Thought,* Cambridge: Cambridge University Press, vol. 1, p. 133.
2. W. Winiarski (1987) 'Machiavelli', in L. Strauss and J. Cropsey (eds) *History of Political Philosophy,* Chicago, Ill: University of Chicago Press, p. 19.
3. Machiavelli (1968) *The Prince,* Harmondsworth: Penguin, p. 29.
4. *The Prince,* p. 77.
5. *The Prince,* p. 101.
7. *The Prince,* p. 101.
8. *The Prince,* p. 100.
9. *The Prince,* p. 97.
10. *The Prince,* p. 95.
11. *The Prince,* p. 91.
12. *The Prince,* p. 130.
13. *The Prince,* p. 133.
14. *The Prince,* p. 102.
15. *The Prince,* p. 134.
16. *The Prince,* p. 135.

17. *The Prince*, p. 133.
18. *The Prince*, p. 100.
19. B. Crick (ed.) (1988) *Discourses on Livy*, Harmondsworth: Penguin, p. 112.
20. *The Prince*, p. 102.
21. *The Prince*, p. 131.
22. *The Prince*, pp. 124–4.

Further reading

Anglo, S. (1969) *Machiavelli*, London: Gollancz.
Butterfield, H. (1955) *The Statecraft of Machiavelli*, London: Bell.
Eldar, D. (1986) 'Glory and the boundaries of public morality in Machiavelli's thought', *History of Political Thought*, vol. VII: 419–39.
Hale, J.R. (1961) *Machiavelli and Renaissance Italy*, London: English Universities Press.
Machiavelli (1968) *The Prince*, Harmondsworth: Penguin.
Machiavelli (1988) *The Discourses* (ed. B. Crick), Harmondsworth: Penguin.
Pitkin, H. (1986) *Fortune is a Woman*, Princeton, NJ: Princeton University Press.
Pocock, J.G.A. (1975) *The Machiavellian Moment*, Princeton, NJ: Princeton University Press.
Price, R. (1988) 'Self-love, "Egoism" and Ambizione in Machiavelli's Thought', *History of Political Thought*, vol. IX: 237–62.
Skinner, Q. (1988) *Machiavelli*, Oxford: Oxford University Press.
Skinner, Q. (1978) *The Foundations of Modern Political Thought*, Cambridge: Cambridge University Press.

6 | HOBBES: WAR AND THE LAWS OF NATURE

Thomas Hobbes was born in the year of the defeat of the Spanish Armada (1588) near Malmesbury, Wiltshire. He is sometimes regarded as the greatest of England's political philosophers. He has a striking style and is always interesting in what he has to say. For part of his life he was tutor to William Cavendish, Earl of Devonshire. In 1626 Hobbes published his translation of Thucydides' *History of the Peloponnesian War,* a descriptive and highly detailed account of the wars between Athens and Sparta in ancient Greece. Some commentators regard this work of Thucydides as one of the earliest tracts in international relations. Hobbes was greatly influenced by the development of mathematical sciences and astronomy in his time. He met and befriended the French materialist philosopher Gassendi and became a materialist philosopher himself. He also travelled on the European continent to meet the famous astronomer Galileo.

His first political treatise, the *Elements of Law,* appeared in 1640. As a consequence of the disturbances brought about by the English Civil War Hobbes fled to France until 1651. In France Hobbes wrote his most famous works, *De Cive* (1642) and *Leviathan* (1651). In 1646 Hobbes had been appointed tutor in mathematics to Charles II, but *Leviathan* was badly received by the court in exile. This estranged him from Charles II for some time. Hobbes returned to Britain under the protectorate of Oliver Cromwell. Ultimately Hobbes was given a pension by Charles II.

Human nature and the nature of politics

In his political philosophy Hobbes gives a great deal of attention to the problem of human nature. A claim that is very often made in everyday political discussion and debate is that you may strive to change institutions as you will, but you will never successfully change human nature. In this sense aspects of human nature often appear as obstacles to much-needed reform. The opinion might be readily expressed that were it not for the cussedness of human nature an objective or goal might easily be achieved. It might also be suggested that no world peace is possible with material as awkward and recalcitrant as humankind.

Not surprisingly, this kind of argument has attracted the attention of political theorists and writers in international relations. Many theorists have expressed the view that the best way to get to the heart of the problems they study is by undertaking a close examination of human nature. In looking at the nature of the human individual, free of all external influence, such theorists think that they may be able to get a sound idea as to the kinds of social and political institutions which are appropriate for governing us. Similar arguments have been used in relation to international society. Kenneth Waltz in his book *Man, the State and War* takes up this line of thought when he examines what he describes as the 'first image' or influential concept which lies behind our thinking about international society. As Waltz puts it, 'according to the first image of international relations, the locus of the most important causes of war is found in the nature and behaviour of man'.[1] Thus the cure to the evils of international society is to be found in the reform of the character of humankind. If people are by nature aggressive, to induce peace their instinctual aggressiveness has to be cured and re-directed into harmonious paths.

Hobbes is perhaps the most remarkable of the state of nature theorists. His approach to the question of the nature of humankind is that of a thoroughgoing materialist. He is, seemingly, brutally frank about what he sees as the essentially egotistical nature of all our motives. He says, 'in the first place, I put for a general inclination of all mankind, a perpetual and restless desire of power after power, that ceaseth only in death.'[2]

Hobbes doesn't think we seek power merely for its own sake. We seek power, he thinks, because it represents a means of acquiring those other things which make life worthwhile. It is through power alone that we can achieve a contented life. This contentment which Hobbes sees as the objective of life he calls felicity.

In saying this Hobbes does not regard himself as moralizing about the human individual. He does not want to impute blame nor otherwise to find fault with our present behaviour. He apparently sees himself as tackling the problem of the nature of the human individual in an objective and scientific manner. Hobbes may well see himself describing the human individual as he believes a dispassionate observer would. And from this point of view there is little doubt in his mind about the fact that nature has made us all equal. Where we may observe physical inequalities among individuals we might sensibly conclude that these are more than made up for by mental capabilities. The physically weak person may achieve by cunning what cannot be achieved by force. The same kind of evasive strategy might be open to weaker states in the international system. Whatever opinion we may hold of another state or person we are unlikely to undervalue our own qualities and abilities to the extent that we do not believe that we are at least the equal of, if not indeed better than, that state or person. Since we see ourselves at first hand and others only at one remove, we are unlikely to underestimate our own powers, whereas the capabilities of others might appear negligible in comparison.

From this view of the human individual as confident, if not arrogant, Hobbes builds up a view of human society. From the optimistic assumption of natural equality there arises, in Hobbes's opinion, an 'equality of hope in attaining our ends'.[3] Through our natural enthusiasm we all have the same expectations of achieving our purposes. However, if any two persons end up wanting the same thing – and given our equal estimation of our own worth – conflict may be the only outcome. This might also be the position of any two states in world society, particularly those with new leaders. Conflict then makes the two into enemies, and this opposition may be overcome only in the state of nature by the use of force. In such a situation – corresponding to what Hobbes understands to be a state of nature – no individuals can be sure of their rights. Whatever one person has may be desired by another, and where there is no third power to decide between them, individuals may stand to lose whatever they have gained.

There are in Hobbes's view in the nature of humans three principal causes of quarrel. 'First, competition: secondly, diffidence; thirdly, glory.'[4] The first makes people disregard the rights of others for gain; the second makes people strike at another as a means of defence (their concern is safety); and the third makes people violate others' liberty 'for the sake of reputation'.[5] Of course, if a situation were to prevail where individuals were allowed to give full rein to these emotions there would be no life at all: a situation would exist where everyone is carefully watching everyone else, trying to anticipate the first false move against them and what is theirs.

This is a condition of complete insecurity. What is missing in this situation is (according to Hobbes) 'a common power' to keep people in awe. What we have here is not a social or civil condition, but a state of war of every individual against every other individual. Hobbes finds this comparison with the state of war an illuminating one. Because whatever applies in the state of war among nations also applies to the state of nature among people. Under such circumstances people live without security other than that which they can provide for themselves. 'In such a condition,' as Hobbes aptly puts it,

> there is no place for industry; because the fruit there of is uncertain: and consequently no culture of the earth; no navigation, nor use of the

commodities that may be imported by sea; no commodious building; no instruments of moving, and removing, such things as may require much force; no knowledge of the face of the earth; no account of time; no arts; no letters; no society; and which is worst of all, continual fear, and danger of violent death; and the life of man, solitary, poor, nasty brutish, and short.[6]

With these well-known words Hobbes provides a powerful picture of a society without government. The picture is almost entirely negative. Conflict is for Hobbes almost always destructive. Perhaps what may account for some of the passion which lies behind this view was Hobbes's recent and vivid experience of the English Civil War. He may well have been depressed by those many vicious and unpleasant acts he saw take place. Although, like many other political theorists Hobbes does not put a great deal of stress on the state of nature having existed historically at some point, he does believe evidence of what people would be like without government can be discovered in contemporary society. Anyone who doubts his view on the state of nature should consider the fact that even when a person knows there are officers of the law to guard him, 'he rides armed', 'locks his doors at night' and does not venture out alone.[7] What can our views of other people be if we feel the need to take all these precautions? Further evidence of people's inclinations in a natural state can be found in the behaviour of savage tribes, untouched by civilization. Hobbes points to the condition of North American Indians in his day. Such people live in a savage and brutish manner, in Hobbes's opinion, and we can envisage what a state of nature might be like if we observe how people of the same nation treat each other in a civil war. And if we are not convinced we might also refer to the condition of international society where again there is no common authority.

Kings, and persons of sovereign authority, because of their independency, are in continual jealousies, and in the state and posture of gladiators; having their weapons pointing, and their eyes fixed on one another; that is, their forts, garrisons, and guns upon the frontiers of their kingdoms; and continual spies upon their neighbours.[8]

Thus with Hobbes there is but one path to peace among people. We have to give up our unhealthy and unpleasant original freedom in order to bring about some kind of security and order. We give up our natural, lawless condition of our own volition recognizing its inadequacies. So the *Leviathan* comes to embody the authority we dare not exercise ourselves. Its power is absolute and beyond question. For Hobbes the sovereign has to be a kind of mortal God which through its absolute power forces individuals to live in harmony with one another. There seems little doubt if Hobbes were to think it in our grasp that it is the same prescription he would make for international society. The only long-term cure for the international state of nature is for the Hobbesian a world *Leviathan*.

This covenant we make with each other to establish a sovereign is – and has to be – a very one-sided affair. There is no recourse to a third party if the *Leviathan* fails to live up to our expectations. Indeed the sovereign incurs no obligation towards the individual who lives under its authority. Those enjoying the peace afforded by Hobbes's sovereign indeed have duties towards the sovereign but the sovereign has no duties towards them. The contracting parties lose their independence in order to be secure.

Many political theorists see this as too great a loss of freedom by the contracting parties. With Hobbes subjugation seems to be the price of civil peace. Others have said the same about a Leviathan controlling international society. World government might well suffocate individual states. John Locke, another well-known political theorist who was a partial contemporary of Hobbes, favours a contract of citizenship in place of Hobbes's covenant of mutual subordination. With Locke's social contract individuals remain free because they recognize the right of others to a regulated autonomy under the authority of a sovereign. Instead of Hobbes's complete loss of natural independence Locke stresses the gaining of social independence. Coercion is never absent from Hobbes's vision of a peaceful society, whereas with Locke coercion exists as a possibility inherent within the social contract, but not necessarily a possibility always in need of enforcement.

How then does Hobbes's model relate in detail to international relations? Present international society is made up of over 150 states who are each in principle free to enact whatever laws they see fit within their territories. Each state is understood to be independent of the other and if the borders, laws or actions of one state are violated by another state this is regarded as contrary both to international law and justice. The situation is summed up in the United Nations Charter (1945) where interference by states in the internal affairs of other states is ruled out. The Charter envisaged that only the UN itself would have authority to act in such a way.

Each state is then in principle a judge in its own case. No other state can try to tell it how to behave. States relate to each other in a way which is directly analogous with Hobbes's view of relations among individuals in a state of nature. In practice, of course, the notion of sovereign independence is undermined by the varying power of states. Big, well-armed states are in a position to suggest to others what to do. Many states belong to international communities or alliances which also limit their freedom of action. The United States and USSR are, in particular, in a strong position to influence the activity of others. Of course, this influence is most marked with the states nearest their borders; however, it is not absent in their relations with smaller states a great distance away. Small states might have to use a great deal of cunning to outweigh the influence of the greater size of these two superpowers.

States in the present international system enjoy then varying conditions of independence. Those with very little resources and consequently poor defence forces potentially enjoy very little. At the other end of the scale the USA and the USSR appear to enjoy a great deal of independence. They at least might be seen as fully sovereign states and therefore as relating to each other in a way similar to that of Hobbes's individuals in a state of nature. And although other states might not enjoy full equality with these two superpowers they may none the less demonstrate a great deal of autonomy in the actions they take, particularly in matters which affect themselves most closely.

Hobbes's frank account of the distrustfulness of natural humankind might not tell the whole story of the potential relation between sovereign states but it might be seen as putting together some interesting possibilities. We are dealing with human calculation and action both at the level of Hobbes's state of nature and at the level of international society. We are discussing comparable states of affairs. And at times it may seem that analogies such as this illuminate a problem in a way that more direct reasoning appears incapable of doing.

An illustration of the power of Hobbes's analogy might be this. Hobbes says of individuals in the state of nature:

> hence it comes to pass, that where an invader hath no more to fear, than another man's single power; if one plant, sow, build, or possess a convenient seat, others may probably be expected to come prepared with forces united, to dispossess, and deprive him, not only of the fruit of his labour, but also his life, or liberty.[9]

In other words, without law and the means of enforcement individuals cannot be sure that what is rightfully theirs remains so. But at times of crisis does not international society appear to be like this? Instances of the uncertainty of possession and the insecurity of international society seem to be: Poland at the time of the Nazi invasion in 1939, Finland at the time of the Nazi–Soviet pact, India in the period of decolonization and the Middle East at the time of British withdrawal. More recently we might cite the collapse of communism in eastern Europe as demonstrating the fragility of peaceful international relations. Below the surface of international society appears to simmer an environment in which the state or group which strikes first has the upper hand. Nothing seems wholly secure. As with Hobbes's state of nature among ungoverned people there is, it seems, a disposition to war in international society.

Hobbes takes the view that in the absence of a mighty power which holds everyone in dread no laws rightly called will exist. Fear is necessary for the regulation of relations among individuals. No 'law can be made, till they have agreed upon the person that shall make it'.[10] Individuals will obey laws for two reasons, the desire of advantage, and the fear of punishment if they fail to obey. But desire of advantage may run contrary to what the rules may require. In which case we have only fear of punishment to fall back on.

Without a common power to give reality to this fear the rule of law will be undermined.

But Hobbes may paint too bleak a picture here. Some of our experience of international society appears to run counter to his view. Although there is no (one) common power, states have from time to time been known to recognize international law. This recognition is not a hard and fast thing: states may flout law where they believe they can get away with it, as, for instance, with the Argentinian invasion of the Falklands and the Iraqi invasion of Kuwait. However, the occasional lapse appears to go hand in hand with a mutual recognition of rules. It appears, then, that Hobbes's state of nature is (at least, as mirrored in international society) not wholly one of continuous war.

Although Hobbes may be misplaced in his most pessimistic moods about the role of law in an ungoverned environment he may have hit the mark in his view of the determining factors that might confront an individual or nation in an environment without enforceable law. In my opinion international society is not wholly in a state of nature as envisaged by Hobbes. In this environment Hobbes thinks that each aims first of all at *self-preservation*. But he does not take a stand in moral judgement over this. He thinks that it is entirely legitimate for each to act in ways which preserve themselves. In accord with this he argues that there are but two fundamental laws of nature: 'seek peace and follow it. The second, the sum of the right of nature; which is, by all means we can, to defend ourselves.'[11]

Hobbes's two fundamental laws of nature represent something of a watershed in the development of political theory. They also represent an important contribution to the theory of international relations. There is a sharp contrast between the priority Hobbes gives to self-preservation and the duty of obedience to the powers that be preached by Augustine and Aquinas. Hobbes regards himself as thoroughly Christian as Augustine and Aquinas but he cannot accept that we can and should put the well-being of the larger society before our own well-being and survival. This is an important shift. If every individual and every state is prepared to fight back rather than submit to force, victory goes not to the traditional authority but the strongest and most determined. Thus, Hobbes's position if reflected in events would give a continuous, possibly frightening, dynamic to world society. States might adjust themselves in relation to each other to the point where they felt they could best survive.

The laws of nature

Laws of nature play an important part in the theory of international society which emerges from Hobbes's political philosophy. This is because Hobbes thinks the laws of nature are identical with the laws of international society.

The law of nations and the law of nature, is the same thing. And every sovereign hath the same right, in procuring the safety of his people, that any particular man can have, in procuring the safety of his body.[12]

At first sight Hobbes seems to be advocating a particularly aggressive doctrine. Just as egoism appears to prevail among individuals in a state of nature so egoism is the overriding motivation in relations among states. It appears that to be prepared to defend yourself at all cost presupposes an insecure environment where no use of force can be ruled out. In preparing to defend oneself then one might have the undesired consequence of creating a more insecure and unstable environment. To be defensive in one's approach to others is to undermine confidence in the social interaction. Defensiveness may inadvertently lead to an attacking disposition in others.

However, the next law of nature which Hobbes derives from his fundamental premises gives a different picture. The first precepts of Hobbes's laws of nature have to be seen in the light of this second law and the further ten or so laws that Hobbes regards emanating from our natural condition. As Hobbes sees it the second law of nature implies:

that a man (or state) be willing, when others are so too, as far-forth, as for peace, and defence of himself he shall think it necessary to lay down his right to all things; and be contented with so much liberty against other men, as he would allow other men against himself.[13]

Thus in an international society which resembles the state of nature we may be prepared to curtail the liberty of action of the state if other states are prepared to do likewise. This rule can be summed up in the concept of reciprocity or in biblical terms as 'do unto others as you would be done by'.

States will renounce their unhindered rights only where they can see some advantage to themselves. At present states within the European community renounce their rights to levy duties on goods imported from other member states on the grounds that other member states will do the same. But there are some rights, it seems, that no individual or state will (reasonably) transfer. A state cannot transfer its right to defend itself when it is attacked by force. The right of self-preservation cannot be transferred. Any state that actually appeared to be transferring this right cannot be taken to have meant it. As Hobbes puts it, 'a covenant not to defend myself from force, by force, is always void'.[14]

Hobbes's laws of nature appear in an even more positive light with his fourth law, 'that a man which receiveth benefit from another of mere grace, endeavours that he which giveth it, have no reasonable cause to repent him of his good will'.[15] If we translate this into terms which concern relations among states we have the valuable precept that where one state acts benevolently towards another the beneficiary should not do anything to undermine this act of friendship. Solicitude should be met by gratitude. We see this precept in force where unforeseen disasters hit one state and this leads other states to offer humanitarian aid. No matter how poor the relation among those states prior to the disaster the expectation is that offers of help will be met with in a co-operative and friendly fashion. As Hobbes remarks, where the desire to co-operate is frustrated there will be 'no beginning of trust'.[16]

Building on the civil acceptance of such gifts and support we have what I regard as further crucial law of nature. Acceptance of this rule may do a great deal to smooth relations among individuals and states. This fifth law of nature is *'complasance;* that is to say, that every man strives to accommodate himself to the rest'.[17] By analogy with this law of nature each state should seek to accommodate itself to others. Aiming at sociability, states should do their best to make their partners feel at ease in the relationship. Each state is no doubt different but it should not act so at variance with others that it finds itself in danger of being cast out of international society. States that step beyond what is required by this rule also put themselves in danger of infringing one of the fundamental precepts of the laws of nature, namely the rule that commands that we should preserve ourselves.

The sixth law of nature is also concerned with co-operation as much as survival. This law of nature requires, 'that upon caution of the future time, a man ought to pardon the offences on the part of them that repenting, desire it'.[18] Seen in terms of international relations this would imply that states which are not prepared to pardon others after a conflict or difference of opinion seem set to persevere in a state of hostility. Equally, those states who only appear to wish to be pardoned are also reserving the right to open up hostilities in the future.

Hobbes accepts that in the state of nature violent conflict will occur, but like those philosophers who have considered the issue of the just war he thinks that violence should not occur in a wholly unregulated and arbitrary manner. Were this to happen it would render the state of nature even more inhospitable than necessary. In consequence the seventh law of nature requires that 'in revenge, i.e., retribution of evil for evil, then look not at the greatness of the evil past, but the greatness of the good to follow'.[19] Revenge upon another state 'without respect to the example, and profit to come, is a triumph, or glorying in the hurt of another'.[20] This is contrary to reason and it will itself tend to war. For Hobbes there is no room for arrogance and vanity in relations among individuals and states in the state of nature. To take pleasure in the hurt of others is itself an offence which does nothing to break the cycle of violence. If we are to create confidence in our mutual relations we have to act wisely and with compassion.

This is a point taken up in the eighth law of nature, which requires that 'no man by deed, word, countenance or gesture, declare hatred, or contempt of another'.[21] No state should actively demonstrate a dislike of another.

Where they do so they create a condition of hostility. This seems to me to be as equally an important rule as the fifth law of nature. It can but help promote peace and mutual understanding among states if political leaders refrain from openly denigrating their opponents. We may find the actions of other states intolerable but it is not sensible or advisable to regard the state itself or its citizens as a whole as intolerable. An example of the value of this principle might be seen in the attitude adopted by enlightened opinion towards Germany in the twentieth century. Hating the German people for the hideous excesses of the Nazis would do nothing to lessen international tension. However despising the actions of certain of their leaders like Adolf Hitler can coexist with a respect for the positive accomplishments of the German people. In dealing with other states we have not to overlook the overriding need to coexist with them. Some of their actions we may justifiably deplore, but if we begin to hate them then we undermine any possibility of co-operation.

The ninth law of nature draws attention to the need for tolerance and co-operation and provides a basis for it. The ninth law requires that 'every man acknowledges another for his equal by nature'. Translated into the terms of international relations this requires that each state should look upon the other as equal to itself in principle. Each must be fit to contract with others as it wishes. As Hobbes puts it in relation to the individual: 'there are very few so foolish, that had not rather govern themselves, than be governed by others'.[22] This principle of sovereign equality is enshrined in the United Nations Charter. It exists as a publicly recognized goal for states and political leaders to achieve. In recognizing the principle I think Hobbes is correct in suggesting that states will be taking a step towards increasing international harmony.

With his tenth law of nature Hobbes outlines another valuable principle that, if observed, would greatly contribute to international harmony. The law requires that 'Once peace is declared no state should enter into it reserving for themselves any right which it is not prepared to grant for others.'[23] In practice this is a very difficult rule to observe. In social life we tend to expect of others that they should not violate our property and our rights, but we tend to be a good deal more lenient or perhaps may even overlook actions of our own that might infringe the rights and property of others. In recent international relations, for instance, the United States may well have wished that the Soviet Union would not interfere in Latin America. The United States might have accepted such renunciation of involvement as a step towards peace. Yet at the same time the United States may well have felt it still had a legitimate interest in Turkey, Pakistan and China (states bordering on the USSR). But, following Hobbes's tenth law, in reserving the right to interfere in these countries the United States might well have undermined the peace it so earnestly desired.

Two final laws which Hobbes outlines are also of some interest to international relations. The eleventh law of nature concerns the distribution of property. Hobbes thinks it sensible where 'things cannot be divided, be enjoyed in common, if it can be; and if the quantity of the thing permit, without stint; otherwise proportionably to the number of them that have right'.[24] This principle seems to have underpinned the use that has been made of Antarctica and possibly may be seen as underlying the treaty on outer space. The final law also seems obviously helpful in terms of promoting peace. This law is that 'all men that mediate peace, be allowed safe conduct'.[25] The United Nations in its peacekeeping operations seems to have benefited from at least the partial acceptance of this rule.

Hobbes and the national interest

What is the main conclusion of Hobbes's international theory? It is (in my view) that there is such a thing as a legitimate national interest which may at times override the common interest. This view derives from Hobbes's discussion of self-preservation. For Hobbes there is always a legitimate self-interest which it is both moral and right to defend. For instance, you ought not to contract with another or conduct yourself in a way that forbids you to defend yourself when threatened. Hobbes is very clear that a threat to your life allows you to act contrary to the interests of others. Society may not wish to preserve your life but you always have a natural right to fight to preserve it. The same applies to a state. 'Every sovereign hath the same right, in procuring the safety of his people, that any particular man can have, in procuring the safety of his body'.[26]

But Hobbes seems to think that what your interests are and what threatens your life are self-evident. Often they are not. Thus you can unwittingly undermine your vital interests. Should a person's vital interests include relatives, partner and friends? What is the cut-off point here? Should a state's vital interests include the well-being of its immediate neighbours? In Hobbes's system individuals end up deciding for themselves where their vital interests lie.

But it is precisely this open-ended nature of self-interest and consequently national interest that makes Hobbes's philosophy so appropriate for the international scene. Here it is clear that each state decides for itself where its interests lie. On the whole states are not expected to prejudice their existence or enter into agreements that are not advantageous to themselves.

Notes

1. K.N. Waltz (1965) *Man, the State and War*, New York: Columbia University Press, p. 16.
2. Hobbes (1969) *Leviathan*, London: Fontana, p. 123.

3. *Leviathan*, p. 142.
4. *Leviathan*, p. 143.
5. *Leviathan*, p. 143.
6. *Leviathan*, p. 143.
7. *Leviathan*, p. 144.
8. *Leviathan*, p. 144.
9. *Leviathan*, p. 142.
10. *Leviathan*, p. 144.
11. *Leviathan*, p. 146.
12. *Leviathan*, p. 309.
13. *Leviathan*, p. 147.
14. *Leviathan*, p. 153.
15. *Leviathan*, pp. 161–2.
16. *Leviathan*, p. 162.
17. *Leviathan*, p. 162.
18. *Leviathan*, p. 162.
19. *Leviathan*, p. 163.
20. *Leviathan*, p. 163.
21. *Leviathan*, p. 163.
22. *Leviathan*, p. 163.
23. *Leviathan*, p. 164.
24. *Leviathan*, p. 164.
25. *Leviathan*, p. 165.
26. *Leviathan*, p. 309.

Further reading

Baumgold, D. (1983) 'Subjects and soldiers: Hobbes on military service', *History of Political Thought*, vol. IV (1): 43–64.
Brown, C.W. (1987) 'Thucydides, Hobbes, and the derivation of anarchy', *History of Political Thought*, vol. VIII (1): 33–62.
Bull, H. (1981) 'Hobbes and international anarchy', *Social Research* **48**: 717–38.
Hanson, D. (1984) 'Thomas Hobbes's highway to peace', *International Organisation* **38**: 329–54.
Hobbes (1969) *Leviathan*, London: Fontana.
Johnston, D.J. (1986) *The Rhetoric of Leviathan*, Princeton, NJ: Princeton University Press.
Klosko, G. and Rice, D. (1985) 'Thucydides and Hobbes's state of nature', *History of Political Thought*, vol. VI (3): 405–10.
McNally, F.I. (1968) *The Anatomy of Leviathan*, New York: St Martin's Press.
Morgenthau, H.J. (1956) *Politics among Nations*, New York: Knopf.
Oakeshott, M. (1975) *Hobbes on Civil Association*, Oxford: Basil Blackwell.
Peters, R. (1956) *Hobbes*, Harmondsworth: Penguin.
Pouncey, P. (1980) *The Necessities of War*, New York: Columbia University Press.
Raphael, D.D. (1977) *Hobbes*, London: Allen & Unwin.
Warrender, H. (1957) *The Political Philosophy of Hobbes*, Oxford: Clarendon Press.

7 | ROUSSEAU: THE IMPOSSIBILITY OF INTERNATIONAL HARMONY

Jean-Jacques Rousseau was born in Geneva in 1712. His mother died when he was ten months old. Rousseau was brought up by his widower father, who is thought, quite naturally, to have spoiled the motherless child. Rousseau was an extraordinarily diverse and prolific writer. He is regarded by some as the intellectual inspirer of the French Revolution, others have seen him simply as an adventurer, novelist and wholly unsystematic thinker. He is reputed to have had a profound influence upon the intellectual development of Kant.

The first of Rousseau's distinguished writings was his *Discourse on the Sciences and the Arts*. This essay was entered for a competition organized by the Academy at Dijon in 1750. Rousseau's second, perhaps more famous, *Discourse on Inequality* was entered for the same prize in 1755. These essays established him as a critical writer of note. In *Emile* and *Julie, ou la nouvelle Héloïse* he turned, with similar success, to the fictional literary form. His major work in political theory the *Social Contract* was published in 1762. His interest in international relations was expressed in essays on the conditions for perpetual peace and his constitutional writings on Corsica and Poland.

Rousseau is a person of stark contrasts. He combined a deep interest in moral concerns with a highly eventful and possibly irresponsible private life. He was both a figure of the Enlightenment and a leading light of the romantic movement. He recommended an active intelligent citizenship but he despaired of the average person's ability to achieve this goal. He was imbued with deeply democratic instincts but with his notion of the general will threatened to undermine democracy in practice. Rousseau is a thoroughgoing critic of all established society, who none the less believes in civic freedom as the only possible road now open to us. With Rousseau I am not always entirely convinced that he has an eye solely to the truth. Often he seems as much concerned with the impact of his ideas on his audience as he is with their accuracy. Like Nietzsche he seems to prefer best of all the truth which shocks.

Humankind's natural condition

We have seen Hobbes describe humankind's natural state in a highly pessimistic way. Outside the discipline of a civil society people find it very difficult, he claims, to get on with each other. The one individual is always prepared to invade the territory of another for gain, security and glory. Unregulated international society is an example to us of what harm the nature individual can bring about. Our motives in a state of nature do not bear close examination. Narrow self-interest is at the heart of all our intentions. As a consequence Hobbes thinks our natural state is one of war of every individual against every other individual.

Rousseau takes a view of our natural state which is the direct opposite of that of Hobbes. He thinks that we are by nature innocent. Yet Rousseau is not wholly optimistic about our natural condition. For Rousseau takes literally the call to look at humankind's original state. He examines closely the condition of humans in their pre-civil state, that is as savages. The savage, for Rousseau, is not a social being, but is both innocent and wholly self-sufficient.[1] Rousseau's view is that Hobbes has unfortunately confused our natural condition with our social condition. Those characteristics that Hobbes imputes to humans in their original condition are in reality the product of our social and historical development.

Because Hobbes dwells on 'wants, avidity, oppression, desires, and pride' he 'has transferred to the state of nature ideas which were acquired in society; so that in speaking of the savage', he inadvertently describes 'the social man'.[2] The greater part of the ills which Hobbes depicts in our supposed natural state are of our own making. The way to have avoided these ills is to have adhered 'to that simple, uniform, the solitary manner of life which nature prescribed'.[3]

So for Rousseau, paradoxically, humankind's least desirable, unsociable qualities are brought into existence by society itself. Greed, selfishness, competition, indifference, pride and the desire for glory are all characteristics which are bred into the humble individual by living with others in a social condition. Hobbes can therefore depict people as being at war with each other in the state of nature because people are in reality enemies in so-called civilized society. For Rousseau the human being is then corrupted by society. The human natural estate is one of innocence. In the state of nature 'the care we take for our own preservation is less prejudicial to that of others'.[4] Consequently it is (in Rousseau's view) the best calculated to promote peace and seemingly the most suitable condition for humankind. Hobbes was wrong to depict the state of nature as one of war.

Following the same line of argument the evils of international society might now be seen as coming about not so much as a result of some innate quality in humankind but rather as a result of the international environment itself. For Rousseau international society would not be in a 'state of society'. In international society we should see writ large the problems of domestic society: factionalism, unbridled pursuit of self-interest, malice and envy.

Rousseau's account of humankind entering into society is (so it seems to me) very much like the biblical account of our fall from grace. Becoming social and political beings is seemingly humanity's original sin. It is our fall from grace which introduces us to all sorts of vices and diseases. For Rousseau it is the earthly city which creates the need for Augustine's contrasting City of God. For in comparison with the evils and sicknesses which characterize society, the human savage condition appears almost utopian. In present society we are like fallen angels condemned to live according to inhuman standards. The solitary, primitive and social life of the savage is from many standpoints far preferable to our civilized conditions.

Perhaps it is this view of human nature which explains the startling views expressed at the beginning of the *Social Contract*. Here Rousseau says, 'Man is born free; and everywhere he is in chains. One thinks himself the master of others, and still remains a greater slave than they'.[5] When Rousseau refers to the chains that are upon us we can easily be misled into thinking that he is referring to the lack of freedom afforded by a certain type of society. It may for instance seem that he is objecting to the kind of absolutist regime to be found in the France of his day. But this is not so. He is objecting to government and society in general. By entering a social condition we deprive ourselves of our original innocence and freedom.

It seems then that Rousseau has no alternative other than to depict all modern society as a dark tyranny which suppresses human natural goodness. But this is not the case. Despite its sombre beginning the *Social Contract* has a positive outlook. For the *Contract* Rousseau hits upon another view of freedom which he finds a satisfactory alternative to our natural, primitive freedom. This is a socialized freedom. Rousseau accepts the inevitability of social organization and proposes what are, he thinks, the best arrangements for securing our independence in such a world.

The question which occupies Rousseau in the *Social Contract* is how is it human individuals come to be in a social condition? For what reasons do people accept social and political restraint as legitimate given that they may well prefer their natural freedom? Rousseau's manner of posing this question appears to emphasize the voluntary nature of our choice to enter society. A voluntary nature that might well accord with the position of states in international society. For Rousseau it seems that the authority society has over individuals – or the chains that bind them – have to be of the individual's own making. If the chains were seen to be imposed by a society of which individuals felt themselves not to be part, this would really be intolerable.

The family is for Rousseau the first model of political societies. All people are part of a family because it is to their own advantage to be so. At the beginning of their lives children would not survive physically without parents. The parents provide them with food, shelter and clothing. As children grow up they learn from their parents those skills (of which language is one) which are essential to social interaction. When the child reaches the age of maturity the need for the family is no longer there. The children are then released from their obedience to the father, and the father is released from the care he owes to his children. Thus the members of the family return to their original independence. For Rousseau this proves that they gave up their liberty in the first place only for their own advantage. In exchange for the concern they show towards their children the parents receive love and respect, and in exchange for love and respect the children receive care. Although a natural institution, then, the family for Rousseau bears the hallmarks of all social institutions: it was constructed for the convenience and advantage of its members.

Rousseau thinks this picture of the role of the family as a natural institution is an uncontentious one. That it is a highly contentious one tells us a great deal about his vision of politics and the contemporary world. I think it would be fair to say that Rousseau is unashamedly rationalistic and modernistic in his political outlook. The individual he sees as potentially a careful consistent and calculated actor. Individuals can clearly discern where their own interest lies and act on that knowledge. In this political outlook people should not be held back by sentimental, romantic or traditionalist notions. The strongest natural tie – that to kith and kin – can be broken when it is sensible to do so. No one owes allegiance to a fellow family member simply because he or she is a family member. (There is no place for the extended family.) No doubt Rousseau would accept that the same principle be applied to national society. He may not see it as sensible to owe allegiance to our fellow citizens simply because they are fellow citizens. So all that does not make sense from the point of view of rational deliberation can be broken asunder. No political arrangements – national or inter-national – are acceptable that do not accord with reason.

Social contract

Political power for Rousseau ought always to be brought into being in favour of those to be governed. The strong have no automatic right to rule over the rest of us on their own behalf. 'Let us then admit that force does not create right, and that we are obliged to obey only legitimate powers'.[6] The whole point about force, Rousseau holds is that it can never on its own establish a right. Rights have to be recognized by the population as a whole and can never be acquired solely by coercing people. It may well be prudent for us to 'obey the power that be', but no government can be made legitimate entirely by such obedience. As with the father in the family the government must earn its respect by showing that it has the best interests of the community at heart.

It may be that Rousseau argues so passionately in favour of authority being established by those who are to be subject to it because in the Europe of his day the opposite was more often the case. It is not difficult for us to see also why his name was so often linked with the acts of the revolutionaries in France in 1789. With that evolution an absolutist government was forced to accept an obligation to the community as a whole. Seemingly, one of the main objectives of the revolutionaries was to establish a popularly accountable government.

Since therefore Rousseau denies that political authority can be derived from force and discards the notion of the divine right of monarchs, he concludes 'that conventions form the basis of all legitimate authority among men'.[7] Domestic and international society can function harmoniously only if they are founded upon the consent of their participants. It appears from his essays on perpetual peace that Rousseau might like an international social contract. But he thinks this difficult, if not impossible, to bring about. He appears to think that states are in a similar position to private individuals in modern society: *private* interest dominates.

Rousseau's social contract is a complicated affair. But as it also supplies the model for his understanding of international society it is useful for us to pursue it here. With the social contract Rousseau not only wants to create a sovereign authority for society but also wants to preserve the individual's civil freedom. Authority should be established on behalf of individual citizens as well as *over* them. Individuals have to be constrained yet also *feel* free: this represents a very tall order for any form of human organization. Rousseau thinks that it can be achieved through individuals' agreeing as to the respects in which they are to be restrained.

The first move Rousseau thinks should be made to establish the kind of sovereignty he favours is that individuals should place all their freedom and property in the hands of a central authority. Individuals do this since they realize that their natural freedom will be undermined anyway by social interaction. Once a sovereign exists with absolute authority over everyone then large parts of an individual's freedom can be returned. We are, for instance, once again allowed to hold property but we recognize that property is held through the good offices of the sovereign.

It might seem that given enough power it will be possible to create Rousseau's social contract at an international level. But there is more to the contract than first meets the eye. The sovereign Rousseau imagines us to hand over our freedom to (domestically) is the combined body of all citizens that this body requires to sustain itself Rousseau calls the *general will*. The general will expresses the *common interest* and Rousseau apparently assumes that this common interest is only *one*. Following the general will it ought (Rousseau thinks) always to be possible to know what is necessary to sustain sovereignty and benefit the totality of the society. So the sovereign that lies behind the social contract is neither one person nor one institution. It is a sense of oneness that Rousseau believes lies within the community.

Creating this sense of unity at a national level would seem to be an extraordinarily difficult task. At an international level the problem would appear to be insoluble. A major difficulty in trying to bring about the contract Rousseau envisages would seem to be the diversity of human (moral) opinion. Individuals tend to have their own view as to what the good of the community as a whole is.

The kind of domestic community that Rousseau sees emerging as a result of his social contract would be in a continual process of change. Since the sovereign is never wholly identified with the government, the government can always be undermined where it fails properly to reflect the will of the people (the sovereign). Rousseau also envisages within his domestic community the existence of factions which may try to undermine the general will. Such factions are always a possibility since each individual in society is free to follow their particular will. The general will emerges from this pursuit of particular interest. To avoid too many clashes between the particular will and the general will, Rousseau asks each individual to think of themselves as both citizens and bourgeois (with particular private interests). Each individual should then curb their own potentially anti-social behaviour.

Rousseau then asks a great deal of the citizen participating in his social contract. It is doubtful whether any individual will wholly match up to the ideal. Most would not be able to constrain their individualistic, bourgeois inclinations to the extent that Rousseau requires. In sinking your lot in with the general will you may lose sight of your own particular will. What makes the model of the social contract practicable at the domestic level is the possibility of punishment. In Rousseau's loaded phrase, individuals who don't live up to the ideal of citizenship should be 'forced to be free'.[8]

The frequent necessity to employ the measure of punishment to reinforce the individual's freedom seems not to have escaped Rousseau. He is under no illusions about the behaviour of individuals. Once in society individuals may become competitive, greedy, spiteful, malicious and manipulative. This can naturally be offset by the development of a sense of duty, but for Rousseau it would be unwise to rely solely on this motive in seeking good social behaviour.

International peace and the problem of defection

Rousseau expects the same kind of behaviour from states in international society. However, states cannot be coerced as easily as individuals so the prospects for even a measure of success in the international arena are not great. The 'rogue' or anarchic state may always get away with its bad behaviour. Other states must then plan for this bad behaviour. Thus an international system develops based upon distrust.

Rousseau's view on perpetual peace is that it is an ideal goal if it could be achieved. But the requirement for a consciously laid out plan demonstrates, in a paradoxical way, the impossibility of achieving the goal. Were states well enough behaved of their own accord there would be no necessity to make arrangements to ensure that they were. Preparing for the worst demonstrates an expectation that the worst might well happen. It is the pursuit of *private* interest which, in Rousseau's opinion, causes the problem. No state is prepared to give up the possibility of gaining individual advantage over the rest, even if this leads to a more stable international environment. States are, unfortunately, inclined to put their particular wills first rather than pay heed to the general will. Rousseau has, therefore, to devise a means whereby states, just like individuals, can be both citizens and bourgeois, both according to the general will yet also preserve the independence of their particular wills.

Rousseau was preoccupied with attaining an international state within Europe. In his day, of course, most of the civilized world was European. Thus in solving the European problem a political theorist would be going a long way towards solving the general problem. That international society extends well beyond the borders of Europe now does not make his proposals any the less interesting. Intriguingly, the problems of combining the activities of the ten European states within the present European Community illustrate the difficulties that Rousseau anticipated would occur. Those states, like Germany and France, that gladly fell in with the European ideal (the 'general will') might find themselves falling victim to the less idealistic member states, like Britain, who seek the advantages of the union without wanting to pay the costs. The difficulty with such a system is that the general level of co-operation is dictated by the level of co-operation practised by the least enthusiastic partner. The effectiveness of the union is constantly in danger of being undermined by the actions of the reluctant partner.

Rousseau wrote two essays on international peace: first, the 'Abstract of the Abbé de Saint-Pierre's Project for Perpetual Peace', and second, the 'Judgement on Saint-Pierre's Project for Perpetual Peace'. He wrote a further, less well-known, essay on the 'State of War'. These essays were all written around the same time in 1756. Hinsley in *Power and the Pursuit of Peace* regards the abstract as a work praising the proposals of Saint-Pierre and the judgement as a more critical piece.[9] Both (in my opinion) are predominantly critical, with the longer abstract perhaps being more historical in its approach.

On the whole Rousseau finds Saint-Pierre's ideas convincing, but he thinks the means that Saint-Pierre recommends for carrying them out naive. Peace cannot simply be instituted, as Saint-Pierre suggests, simply through a debate or an international conference. Saint-Pierre's approach to international peace seems somewhat similar to that taken by Robert Owen in his pursuit of socialism in the nineteenth century. Owen set out a number of grand plans for the reform of English society, but none came to fruition since all Owen felt it was necessary to do was to give publicity to his ideas and invite parliament to enact the appropriate laws! Owen overlooked the possibility that people's convictions might flow from their actions, rather than their actions flowing from their convictions. Practices are perhaps best changed by new practices.

In the two essays on peace Rousseau puts the case for a European federal government. The Judgement is less positive on the project than the Abstract. Whereas the Abstract outlines the peace proposals in great detail, in the Judgement Rousseau looks closely at all the reasons why he thinks the plan won't work.

There are five points to the plan as Rousseau presents it. Rousseau first envisages that all the sovereign powers of Europe will create a permanent alliance. This alliance should be formed as though the participants were going to fight a war together. But the common enemy would now not be a foreign power, but war itself. The alliance's campaign for peace would be waged in an assembly or parliament where representatives of each state would be sent to discuss those issues which might stand in the way of peace and stability. In order for it to be effective it would have to be made clear from the start that this was an alliance that could not be dissolved. Just like the internal social contract which creates the state, the state in joining the alliance would be giving up its natural freedom. In this light it is interesting that Rousseau proposes an alliance rather than one composite power or sovereign that would immediately obliterate the separate powers. In this respect the international compact would be different from the domestic social contract. Initially at least the distinctiveness of the member states would be respected, although the long-term goal would be political as well as military sovereignty.

As a second step it would be necessary to stipulate the number of sovereigns who would participate in the Congress established by the peace treaty. The object of deciding membership in this way would be to establish how the costs of the confederation would be borne and how the executive responsibilities would be shared. Equally important would be determining who should occupy the role of President and for how long.

As a third step the Confederation should guarantee to 'each of its members the possession and government of all the dominions' which they hold 'at the moment of the Treaty, as well as the manner of succession to them'.[10] This is a very important provision of Rousseau's plan, designed to remove any immediate causes of conflict and aggression. Accepting existing sovereign powers and state boundaries would represent a remarkable step forward. Rousseau did not require that states entirely give up their claims but simply that they gave up the intention of settling them by force.

The fourth clause in Rousseau's peace compact concerns the actions to be taken about anyone who breaks the Treaty. 'All the confederates shall arm and take the offensive, conjointly and at the common expense, against any state put to the ban of Europe'.[11] States who break the terms of the treaty shall be regarded as outcasts and cannot be re-admitted to its terms until they have been properly punished and atoned for their errors. Implausible though this condition sounds, not least in the manner of its enforcement, we still have to consider the fate of Germany in the twentieth century. Without any formal treaty most of the states of Europe eventually came round to punishing the anarchic and imperialistic actions of the German state. And it may be the case in the 1990s that with the collapse of the Warsaw Pact Europe may be driven to the kind of Grand Alliance that Rousseau envisaged. 'And it is clear that the Grand Alliance, being perpetually armed and concerned for action, will find no difficulty in forestalling and crushing in advance any partial and seditious alliance'.[12] For Rousseau even in the eighteenth century conquests cost more than they are worth.

This clause in Rousseau's compact is most reminiscent of the Collective Security arrangements of the United Nations. Unfortunately, the example of these arrangements being put into effect is not wholly a good one. The 'uniting for peace' declaration of the United Nations which took place at the time of the Korean War demonstrates the less than impartial use to which collective security arrangements can be made subject. Taking advantage of the absence of the Soviet Union from the Security Council combined measures were taken by the UN against North Korea. Historians have rightly cast doubt over the justice of this action. The declaration may in hindsight have allied the United Nations too closely with the prosecution of United States' foreign policy. But one bad example of the working of a collective security arrangement does not undermine the whole concept. The United Nations has also acted successfully in bringing disputes to an end.

The fifth provision of Rousseau's compact concerns the executive functions of the united powers. Each delegate of the member state to the united executive should be given full sovereign powers.[13] Rousseau envisages that to get the compact off to a good start the united executive should be able to act on the basis of majority support. Gradually as the member states became more used to the Confederation this requirement of a majority could be increased to a three-quarters vote. Both of these arrangements make the position of minority states somewhat vulnerable. The requirement for a preponderance of votes of any kind takes the emphasis off the pursuit of a possible consensus. Finally, it is also interesting to note that the voting arrangements of the Council of

Ministers of the present European Community followed the opposite path to that of Rousseau. The European Community began with total unanimity and is now moving towards majority voting. Majority voting is not of course incompatible with the pursuit of consensus.

If we look at international society as it presently is all we can observe is, according to Rousseau, a continual tale of woe. First, there is no settled law and in its absence the stronger is most likely to prevail. Second, the political situation is always uncertain. Some say that a balance of power develops which deals with the situation. But any balance can of its nature be only temporary. Third, because of the continuous external conflict states experience, the possibility of internal harmony and unity is undermined. Fourth, because of the vastness and diversity of international society there is no point at which you can be certain that you have completely defeated your opponents. Fifth, since every state will have its potential enemies it has always to devote a part of its national income to defence and has continually to be in a position of preparedness for war. Sixth, with an insecure international environment the internal environment is also rendered insecure. A state stands always to be potentially weakened by internal revolt. Seventh, there can be no absolute guarantee that international agreements need be honoured. Since no adequate means of punishment are available states, if they are prepared to flout international opinion, can break agreements. Eighth, as there is no means of enforcing agreements states whose interests have been harmed have no means of ensuring that they obtain justice from their aggressors. Ninth, since the international environment is a dangerous one, and internal politics is similarly precarious, the lives of political leaders are constantly under threat. The Princes of Europe need to watch for their personal security as much as they do for the security of their nations. Tenth, in such an unsure international environment even the state which is internally secure runs the risk of being drawn into the conflicts of others. Neutrality is a difficult path to follow. Eleventh, conflict leads to economic disruption, and this at a time when states can least afford it. Twelfth, a small state will find itself constantly under pressure from a larger neighbour, while a large powerful state may find itself subject to attacks from powerful alliances. Finally, to complete the picture, Rousseau thinks that given the insecurity of the whole, states may just as well throw caution to the winds.[14] For what is there to be cautious about if there is no clearly prudent path to follow? A state will wisely fall back on the pursuit of private interest if no common interest can possibly emerge.

Rousseau does not ask that people should alter their personalities for his plan to work. He believes his plan will work for individuals as they are, 'unjust, grasping and taking their own interest above all things'. If, in spite of all the compelling reasons for its realization, the project fails 'that is not because it is utopian; it is because men are crazy, and because to be sane in a world of madmen is in itself a kind of madness'.[15]

Rousseau's conclusion on the prospects for world peace is a tragic one. The goal is a wholly rational one which is in the interests of everyone. But because it is not in the interests of one state or one individual in particular it is unlikely that true progress can be made. States are condemned by their own self-love to a kind of hell. 'The truth is that the severest penalty of excessive self-love is that it always defeats itself, that the keener the passion the more certain it is to be cheated of its goal'.[16] Each state is given sovereign independence, but this itself is the obstacle to reform. With sovereign states there can be no international accord. For the reign of law is substituted the reign of chance. 'Like a madcap pilot who, to show off his idle skill and his power over his sailors, would rather toss to and fro among the rocks in a storm than navigate his vessel in safety'.[17] Rousseau poses the problem of international politics in its starkest possible form. How are we to obtain peace when that is in the interests of everyone, yet it is in everyone's individual interest to take advantage of that peace for their own selfish ends?

Notes

1. R.D. Masters (1979) *The Political Philosophy of Rousseau*, Princeton, NJ: Princeton University Press, p. 119.
2. Rousseau (1968) *A Discourse on the Origin of Inequality*, in *The Social Contract and Discourses*, trans. G.D.H. Cole, London: Dent, p. 161.
3. *Origin of Inequality*, p. 167.
4. *Origin of Inequality*, p. 181.
5. *Social Contract*, p. 3.
6. *Social Contract*, p. 6.
7. *Social Contract*, p. 7.
8. *Social Contract*, p. 15.
9. F.H. Hinsley (1967) *Power and the Pursuit of Peace*, Cambridge: Cambridge University Press, p. 46.
10. 'Abstract of the Abbé de Saint-Pierre's Project for Perpetual Peace', in M.G. Forsyth, H.M. Keene-Soper and P. Savigear (eds) (1970) *The Theory of International Relations*, London: Allen & Unwin, p. 143.
11. 'Abstract of the Project for Perpetual Peace', p. 143.
12. 'Abstract', p. 145.
13. 'Abstract', p. 144.
14. 'Abstract', p. 155.
15. 'Abstract', p. 156.
16. 'Judgement on Saint-Pierre's Project for Perpetual Peace', in *The Theory of International Relations*, p. 158.
17. 'Judgement', p. 158.

Further reading

Charvet, J. (1972) *The Social Problem in the Philosophy of Rousseau*, Cambridge: Cambridge University Press.

Forsyth, M.G., Keene-Soper, H.M. and Savigear, P. (eds) (1970) *The Theory of International Relations*, London: Allen & Unwin.

Fralin, R. (1986), 'Rousseau and community: the role of moeurs in social change', *History of Political Thought*, vol. VII (1): 131–50.

Hall, J.C. (1973) *Rousseau*, London: Macmillan.

Hinsley, F. (1967) *Power and the Pursuit of Peace*, Cambridge: Cambridge University Press.

Masters, R.D. (1968) *The Political Philosophy of Rousseau*, Princeton, NJ: Princeton University Press.

Roosevelt, G.G. (1987), 'A reconstruction of Rousseau's fragments on the state of war', *History of Political Thought*, vol. VIII: 225–44.

Rosenfeld, D. (1987) 'Rousseau's unanimous contract and the doctrine of popular sovereignty', *History of Political Thought*, vol. VIII (1): 83–110.

Rousseau (1968) *Social Contract*, London: Dent.

8 | KANT: THE IDEA OF PERPETUAL PEACE

By any standards Kant is a major international theorist. Indeed in so far as it is possible to speak of a history of international political theory Kant would have to be regarded as one of its founders. Of the principal philosophers Kant is the exception in that he devotes his most significant writing in political theory to international issues. *Perpetual Peace* (first published in 1795) is an important work of political theory dealing with the main topics of the subject, such as the nature of the state, the nature of humanity, the conditions for political obligation and the best form of the state. However, unlike many previous works in political theory it takes as its focus the question of relations among states. For Kant the problems of internal political order and external political relations cannot be separated.

Immanuel Kant was born in Königsberg, East Prussia, in 1724. Political boundaries have shifted to such an extent since Kant's day that Königsberg is now Kaliningrad in the Soviet Union. Kant's father was a saddler. Kant's mother was of similar humble origins and of a very devout personality. His parents were adherents of the Pietist movement, a revivalist Christian protestant movement similar to the Methodism which took root in Britain in the same century.[1] Kant's poverty meant that he was able to entertain the thought of an academic career as the result of the sponsorship he received from educationalists in Konigsberg who recognized his talents. Even then Kant endured many years of great poverty, first as a private tutor and subsequently as a private teacher (Dozent) at the University of Königsberg, before finally becoming a full professor in 1770.

Kant owes his great fame as a philosopher to his critical system. This system was outlined in a trilogy: first, *The Critique of Pure Reason* (1781): second, *The Critique of Practical Reason* (1788); third, *The Critique of Judgement*

(1790). The object of Kant's critical system was to set limits to the employment of reason. Kant felt that philosophers in the past had been too optimistic about the capacity of human reason. He felt that nothing could be known in its objective totality. Indeed the known world was itself partially (if not fully) the product of human understanding. For Kant the worlds which we could most accurately and most helpfully speak of philosophically were the world of human moral practice and the world of human taste. This conclusion was reflected in the concentration of his two later *Critiques* where he subjects morality and religion (second *Critique*) and aesthetic judgement (third *Critique*) to close examination.

Individuals and progress

The notion of the fallibility of human reason provides a good clue to the tenor of Kant's political philosophy and his approach to international society. We cannot aspire for perfection in human society and politics. Reason can guide our motives in acting but we must not expect the world to correspond wholly to its demands. Human society may improve as a result of a process of trial and error. Reason for Kant has its greatest scope in affecting our wills. Even where events make it difficult we should try to ensure that our actions are guided by reason. Although there may not be one impersonal reason which accounts for the universe of nature, it may be possible for us to approximate to an impersonal reason concerning human actions. Our potential for rationality may draw us together in terms of our actions. But this is always only a possibility, never an inevitability.

Important in understanding Kant's political theory and his view of international society is his philosophy of history. Kant was encouraged to write on the topic of universal history by other academics who wanted to see how his ideal of a perfect civil constitution for each state might be realized.[2] The essay (first published in 1784) is entitled 'Idea for a Universal History with a Cosmopolitan Purpose'. As with all his shorter writings on politics and society, Kant affects to treat the problem of history in a light-hearted way. He sets no great store by the movement of history, but feels that we might have some cause for optimism. Kant systematically excuses this optimism in terms of the necessarily subjective nature of our under-standing of the world. We cannot know for certain how the world is constituted in itself, but we can speak with greater precision about our comprehension of it. We may wish, for moral reasons, to see history as progressing even though factually this may be impossible to prove.

Individual political actors may not have progressed as their aim. Indeed they may well be driven by the most base of ambitions, yet the combined effect of their actions might still be progressive. Kant thinks human beings are possessed of an 'unsociable-sociability'.[3] By this he means that not only do we love to be with others but also we love to separate ourselves from them. Our best qualities develop only in co-operation and competition with our fellow human beings, and to enjoy the warmth and reassurance of others we need their company. Yet we are also fond of our own company. All these pressures are also found at the level of international society. States both need and distance themselves from each other.

In terms of internal politics Kant is a reformer and a gradualist, favouring the division of powers and a representative system. The interests of the state and the interests of the individuals who work for it should be kept separate. There is a strong strain of realism in his approach. Where the liberal ideal of a free and equal society under law he sets out cannot be achieved Kant's motto is to accept the order you already have and work with it to achieve improvements. Kant takes for granted that women and any men without property cannot be full citizens. There is nothing to prevent a state from being governed in a republican manner even though it has an autocratic or monarchical constitution.

Kant has great objections to a paternalist society.[4] Society should not be seen as one giant family where there is a common conception of happiness to be achieved. Under a civil constitution Kant thinks that individuals ought to have the right to seek their own happiness in whatever way they see fit. He ought not to be made to accept somebody else's conception of his welfare. Kant then would find unhelpful any regime which had a strong element of personal power. Charismatic leadership would seemingly not appeal to him. Under no condition should we hand over to the state the right 'to decide in what our happiness consists'.[5] The worst kind of despotism might emerge from acting on the citizen's behalf in matters concerning his or her welfare.

In achieving his reformist goals Kant thinks that an important role can be played by a particular kind of politician. That kind of politician is a moral one.[6] Kant does not see this is an imprudent kind of leadership. For him to act morally is also to act rationally. Moral politicians work in an environment where they are surrounded by competing and even conflicting claims and interests. This concept of a moral politician is intended to contrast with Machiavelli's concept of the amoral prince. Kant thinks that political leaders who looked ultimately to expediency in deciding their policy will ultimately be found out by their people and the leaders of opposing states. Kant is deeply conscious that the political sphere is greatly conditioned by considerations of prudence and strategy. Yet the moral politician is not entirely drawn into this whirlpool of ambition and power-seeking. Other politicians can be made to serve moral purposes behind their backs. At the prudential level Kant thinks there is no sure and certain policy for the unscrupulous politician to adopt, while the moral politician always has a sure guide to action. Prudence must be made to match with the larger goal of justice. In this, Kant finds himself at odds with Aristotle.

There are difficulties that Kant's reforming, moral politician has to face.

Politicians following the path that Kant recommends would be predictable in their actions, and would therefore be more vulnerable to calculated intervention than the unprincipled politician. For instance, if an enemy knows for certain that you will not bomb civilian targets, they can enforce a change in your policy if you are not prepared to go so far. You cannot ensure that politicians first become moral before you deal with them. As an alternative to Kant's morally rigorous approach maybe it is best first to be prudent and then, once security is established, act according to principle.

Kant places as much emphasis upon international relations as domestic relations in his writings on politics. He has a fully developed theory of international relations based upon his view of history and the nature of humankind. He takes the view that domestic politics and international politics are intimately interlinked: the international political problems of states cannot be resolved until their external relations are properly in order. For Kant creating properly organized external relationships takes precedence over the resolution of domestic disharmony. As he puts it in his essay 'Idea for a universal history',

> the problem of establishing a perfect civil constitution is subordinate to the problem of a law-governed external relationship with other states, and cannot be solved unless the latter is also solved.[7]

How does Kant see the human individual? For Kant we are the inhabitants of two different worlds: the world of reason and the world of nature. We have a tendency both to act in an animal-like way and also a tendency to act in a way governed by reason. Our animal selves are unstable, as prone to hatred as to love, kind, yet potentially violent. Above all, the animal self is controlled by nature and not by law. In contrast the thinking self is moved by principles and argument. The rational self deliberates and is capable of acting morally. What is distinctive about moral action is that it is governed by rules which, if they can be generalized, we can call laws.

Kant believes that these two sides of the individual are always in conflict with one another. At times the animal side can gain the upper hand. However, if we are to act virtuously the rational side must be allowed to gain the upper hand. Evidence of our animal side is the conflicts and wars which continually bedevil international relations. Statesmen allow their politics to be governed by appetite and fear rather than law. But for Kant, when we do not act on principle we are not free.

Because human beings suffer from an 'unsociable-sociability' they both need and dislike the company of others. We are competitive and co-operative. Kant thinks that our competitive, grasping side can none the less contribute inadvertently to human progress. Paradoxically, our competitiveness can force ourselves into greater sociability with others. In order to get ahead of others we have, first of all, to be with others. 'All the culture and art which adorn mankind and the finest social order man creates are fruits of his unsociability'.[8] The great artists of the Renaissance – da Vinci, Raphael and Michaelangelo – strove to outdo one another. The same is the case with the advanced nations of the world. Moved on by envy, pride and love of ostentation they strive to out-perform each other economically, militarily and in terms of civil freedom. Internally the leaders of the USSR may not wish civil freedom – but to compete with the west they may feel forced to grant more.

Kant thinks that even wars may be seen as a positive light as 'nature's' way of encouraging states to live in peace with each other. They may convince citizens through their very horror and cruelty of the advantages of living in peace with each other. Wars also lead to a need to regulate relations among states. International law is a product as much of the desire to spell out the rights of combatants in war as the desire to regulate the peaceful relations of states. Treaties signed at the end of a war also help create a regulated international order.

Underlying international law is for Kant a notion of world community. It presupposes that the present international situation, fraught as it is with conflict among very many sovereign states, is only a provisional state of affairs.[9] Although such a world community is a practice very far from being achieved states have to presuppose some common interest if they are to get along with each other in any respect. At the extreme, territories and subjects are held by force. However, if this were so on a day-to-day basis states might well have to devote the whole of their national product to defence. The practicalities of international life dictate that, for the most part, territories and subjects are held through a mutual recognition of right. In imperilling this mutual recognition of right states imperil their own existence. State boundaries would have no meaning were there not some recognition of the notion of a world community.

Kant thinks this world community should be seen as a potential to be realized in the future. Respectable Kantian states will do nothing that will undermine the eventual attainment of this goal, and where circumstances arise where its progress may be advanced they should take advantage of those circumstances. Whereas Hobbes outlines laws of nature which may help a state survive in the international system, Kant takes the more positive line of suggesting rules which may help states continually to live in peace with one another. These rules Kant calls *permissive laws*. Kant is well aware of the difficulties of his task: he thinks there are forces that may favour the success of his project. In particular, he thought that the power of states and the ferocity of their arms might develop to such an extent that the prospect of mutual extinction would lead them into sociability with one another.[10]

World trade might also help found the idea of an international community. Not only does it bring states into contact with one another but also it is of mutual advantage. Trade is disrupted by conflict and war. The price of discord becomes ever greater as the economies of the world become more international.

Agenda for peace

The preliminary articles of Kant's treaty for perpetual peace are sketched in terms of drawing out the potential forces of world community rather than instituting an enforced peace. They represent guidelines rather than dogmatically asserted rules.

1 No conclusion of peace shall be considered valid as such if it was made with a secret reservation of the material for a future war.
2 No independently existing state, whether it be large or small, may be acquired by another state by inheritance, exchange, purchase or gift.
3 Standing armies will be gradually abolished altogether – citizens' armies.
4 No national debt shall be contracted in with the external affairs of a state – borrowing to prosecute a war.
5 No state shall forcibly interfere in the constitution and government of another state.
6 No state of war with another shall permit such acts of hostility as would make mutual confidence impossible during a future time of peace. Such acts would include the employment of assassins or poisoners, breach of agreements, the instigation of treason within the enemy state, etc.[11]

In outlining these preliminary articles Kant introduces the notion of permissive laws. They appear to be somewhat similar in conception to Hobbes's laws of nature. Kant means by permissive laws ones which need not be brought into effect immediately so long as their ultimate objective is not overlooked. Hobbes similarly thought with his laws of nature that even though it might not be possible to realize them immediately they could have a form of existence as motives underlying the actions of statesmen.

Kant does not see articles 1, 5 and 6 in a wholly permissive sense. These are 'laws of nature' that we might immediately seek to enforce if we are serious about peace. Kant thinks that Article 5 is particularly important in this respect. The independence and sovereignty of other states has to be respected. The refusal of one state to recognize the right of another to determine its own fate can only be the cause of continual friction and tension. This principle, it seems, has been an important motive in the withdrawal of the USSR from eastern Europe. The Soviets apparently found the stress placed upon themselves in holding down the states of eastern Europe was not worth whatever benefits that might be regarded as accruing from it. For Kant states ought to relate to each other just as independent individuals relate to each other within civil society. With such mature individuals where one person is regarded as taking a wrong course of action and that action is legal it is not regarded as legitimate to intervene.

As adults we have to accept the right of others to choose the course of action they see fit. In being free and independent ourselves it is furthest from our wish to place another under our tutelage.

With article 6 it appears that Kant does not expect states immediately to lay down their arms and settle their differences. Rather he seems to expect that where conflict does ocur, it should be engaged in such a way that does not undermine the possibilities for future peace. Kant would like the leaders of states to recognize that war is the abnormal condition and so the use of extravagantly unfair methods such as the use of assassins and external subversion should be ruled out. In this respect article 6 falls in with article 1 which stresses that peace treaties should be openly and honestly concluded. In terms of Kant's vision it is perhaps better not to conclude a peace treaty at all than produce one which obfuscates dangerous differences of opinion.

Kant looks upon articles 2, 3 and 4 in a more permissive light. This is particularly the case with article 3. Kant acknowledges that circumstances do not at present favour the abolition of professional armies. Yet this does not prevent the idea of organizing a citizens' militia from being taken up. In the first instance the two types of force might exist side by side. But Kant thinks that it would be more conducive to peace if the citizens' militia gradually replaces the professional machine. Kant's grounds for saying this are persuasive. Members of a citizens' army would not have a strong direct interest in the persistence of war. Indeed their interests might run in the opposed direction of seeking peace in order to pursue their normal activities. Machiavelli likes citizens' armies because they fight with most conviction and determination, Kant likes them because they fight only when they need to.

The reason Kant gives for objecting to external rule in the second preliminary article is that he believes that no state should be treated as property to be owned or exploited by another state. For Kant states should be seen like trees which have their own roots and a tendency of development all of their own.[12] The universally recognized independence of states should be the basis for world peace since this meets the requirement of the original social contract founding the national state. Citizens must be regarded as masters of their own destiny.

Kant's view of the important instrumental role of money in modern warfare leads him to suggest in article 4 that no state should be allowed to increase its national debt in order to prosecute its external policy. By means of increasing the size of the national debt states have at their disposal too simple and effective a means for preparing for and engaging in war. If states are to fight wars Kant thinks that they should be obliged to do so on the basis of their current wealth and income. They should certainly not be able to offset it against future income. States that borrow to prosecute wars are seemingly in a position similar to the gambler who in order to pursue his passion for risk to greater extents takes out an enormous loan. In having to pay now for its armed engagements a state will know its true costs and therefore a decision to open hostilities will less lightly be taken. The economic costs of war represent a severe restraint upon its prosecution. Kant wants to maximize the effect of this constraint.

This preliminary article is a very difficult one to fulfil. In practice it would be extremely hard to detect where the funds for a war originated. Most present-day states have large national debts and many fund an element of their public expenditure on the basis of borrowing. Thus it is extremely likely that the national debt would increase at the time of war, and not necessarily as a result of expenditure on military materials. Kant possibly means that this rule should apply as a subjective test for policy-makers before engaging in hostilities. A political leader who wishes to engage in war should be made to consider if the war will be worth fighting even if it has to be paid wholly from current national income.

Following on these six preliminary articles Kant outlines three definitive *Articles for Perpetual Peace.*

1 The civil constitution of every state shall be republican.
2 The right of nations shall be based on a federation of free states.
3 Cosmopolitan right shall be limited to a condition of universal hospitality.[13]

Although Kant accepts that progress in world society may occur through a natural process he does favour all the same formal agreements to institute a condition of lasting peace. The natural condition of states is, as Hobbes suggests, just like the natural condition of humans before they enter society: it is a permanent condition of insecurity. Thus the founding of a just international order has, from Kant's viewpoint, a great deal in common with the founding of civil society. To achieve a lasting peace states have to give up their arbitrary, natural freedom and accept in its place a self-regulated, lawful freedom. But they will be sufficiently mature to achieve this only when their internal constitutions coincide with the notion of rational freedom based upon law.

We can judge if we are free in this sense only when we can say of our state that it possesses laws to which I can regard myself directly or indirectly as giving consent. This occurs only under a republican constitution. For Kant a republican constitution has two essential features. First, the laws are made by the people's representatives, that is there exists a chamber of deputies or members of parliament which legislate for the state as a whole. Second, within the state institutions themselves there exists a division of powers between the executives and the legislature. The clearest example of such a constitution is probably that of the United States. The nationally elected President, who is the head of the armed forces and appoints the members of the Supreme Court, is subordinate to the law-making body, Congress.

The separation of powers and popular representation provides a powerful lever of control over governments. In a state with a republican constitution those who have to bear the brunt of the financial and human costs of war have the power to decide whether or not they wish to prosecute the war. This right of declaring war was further enshrined as a power of the congress in the United States in the early 1970s. This stress on the right of the people would probably meet with Kant's strong approval.

The next and possibly the most important step in ensuring world peace is outlined by Kant in his second definitive article. This step is that 'the law of nations should be founded on a federation of free states'.[14] Kant puts great stress on the fact that the federation he has in mind would not be the same thing as an international state. On the basis of experience it would seem that such an international state is not possible. Such a state would be too large for one government to rule competently. With any institution the more remote its outer extent the less effective will its administration be. When the number of particulars to which we have given our attention multiplies then our indifference towards each particular grows. In place of the ineffective power of a world state there would arise the power of local agencies of self-protection. Ultimately these local agencies would come to threaten and undermine the central government itself. We can see something of the kind happening in the USSR in the 1990s. Because of its sheer size the control of the centre over the periphery unavoidably declines.

Yet although an international state is an unrealizable ideal 'the political principles which have this aim, those principles namely which encourage the formation of international alliances designed to approach more and more closely the idea'[15] are feasible. Kant's purpose in his essay on peace is to encourage the gradual drawing together of independent nations into one international organization without sovereign powers, as the best approximation to an international state.

Achieving even the minimum of success in developing an international morality depends upon the statesman having as an ideal the goal of a peaceful and harmonious world. Even if in the light of our present circumstances the goal seems unattainable in the absence of the use of force we can regard international arrangements as holding only because we assume the possibility of one world order. And even with the outbreak of war states often try to present their motives in terms of right. In the Falklands conflict, for instance, both Britain and Argentina appealed to international law in defending their actions. Kant would be encouraged by this. That states try to formulate their claims and counter claims in terms of law even at times of war does suggest that they envisage a possible rightful world order.

Lasting peace has to be achieved through the consent of states and their citizens, so what Kant has in mind is a gradually expanding peaceful federation of states. This federation need not enjoy full sovereign powers over its constituent members. Indeed (if I understand Kant correctly) such full powers might be harmful to the realization of the final goal. The object of the federation is rather to safeguard the independence and maintain the security of the individual states. Kant does not see the step from international anarchy to world federation as one analogous with the departure of people from the state of nature. The transition from the state of nature to civil society takes place once and for all through the use of force. Such an approach would not be effective in world society. The means of achieving such an immediate leap would be horrendous. World revolution would destroy more than it would cure. Tyranny might well be its consequence. In contrast with this drastic approach Kant favours gradualism. States should be encouraged to join a peaceful federation of their own volition. In this respect Kant was probably greatly encouraged by the US system, which was unfolding at the time.

This gradualist view has a strong appeal. However, it does invite the rejoinder: how long is a reasonable time to wait for change for the better? Following Kant's perspective the lifetime of one individual might be too short to register any recognizable progress. And if a task is approached gradually and publicly it does allow those individuals and groups which stand to lose from it to organize against its possible success. Kant's approach seems almost too sceptical about human powers. If the goal of world peace has to be approached so circumspectly and slowly are we ever likely to attain it? Ultimately Kant ties up the possible achievement of the goal with the question of human improvement. It is the nature of humankind which stands in the way of progress. As the character of individuals improve so also will the hopes for peace. But what if human character is inextricably linked with circumstances and it is hostile circumstances that gives rise to bad character? Kant would try to avoid this question by saying that if world peace is not possible it is we who fail. We cannot take refuge in the excuse that circumstances got the better of us.

In the third and final definitive article Kant demonstrates that what lies behind his search for international peace is his belief in the essential unity and equality of humankind. 'The law of world citizenship should be limited to the requirements of universal hospitality'.[16] By universal hospitality Kant means that every visitor to another territory should be treated with respect and consideration. Visitors should not be treated with suspicion or with hostility. If world harmony is to exist, we should accept the presence of other races and nations on the earth and welcome them to our state. In assuming the fundamental equality of all human beings, regardless of nationality, race or religion we undermine any justification we might have for placing another race under our power. At the end of *Perpetual Peace* there are two secret articles which provide a strong clue as to the frame of mind in which Kant puts forward his proposals. There is some irony in that Kant presents these articles as secret ones, since he strongly believed in open government. Indeed the second article is directed at attaining the widest possible public debate of foreign policy issues.

Unlike Plato, Kant does not feel that philosophers should rule so that harmony may be brought to the world. Kant believes that the use of power inevitably brings with it a perspective which is at odds with the principle of objective inquiry. Political leaders unavoidably focus on what is of technical relevance to them at the time at issue. In contrast the academic puts no artificial limitations on the sphere of inquiry. Academics consider the possibility that their views might be entirely mistaken.[17]

What Kant asks is that in a civil society the voice of the philosopher should be heard and possibly heeded. Political leaders should welcome their free inquiries since it may provide them with a source of information not directly open to them. A wise ruler encourages the widest possible debate of social and political issues, provided this debate is carried on in a spirit of non-resistance to executive authority. Philosophers must confine themselves to making suggestions on which they may expect the executive to act. But should the executive not heed their advice philosophers have none the less to accept the legitimacy of the actions ensuing. Least of all should philosophers encourage acts of opposition among those who are not authorized to act politically. Policy should be formed in an atmosphere of publicity. Kant thinks that if political leaders cannot make public the motives lying behind their action then those actions may well be wrong. The political leader must seek consent in deciding policy.

The second secret article concerns what Kant regards as the guarantee of progress towards the goal of world peace. Kant feels, probably rightly, that he cannot rely on the human will alone, particularly the wills of political leaders. Yet he thinks improvement can genuinely be aspired to since the actions of states and the constraints imposed by nature will eventually force humankind towards peaceful ways. War itself may become the greatest weapon of peace. The fear of destruction and the devastation of our environment may force humankind to contemplate the seemingly impossible – lasting peace.

Notes

1. H. Williams (1983) *Kant's Political Philosophy*, Oxford: Basil Blackwell; New York: St Martin's Press, p. 27.
2. L.W. Beck (ed.) (1989) *Kant's Selections*, London and New York: MacMillan, pp. 415f.
3. H. Reiss (ed.) (1977) *Kant's Political Writings*, Cambridge: Cambridge University Press, p. 44.
4. *Kant's Political Philosophy*, pp. 131–2.
5. *Kant's Political Philosophy*, p. 130.
6. *Kant's Political Writings*, p. 118: 'And I can indeed imagine a *moral politician*, i.e.

someone who conceives of the principles of political expediency in such a way that they can coexist with morality.'

7. *Kant's Political Writings*, p. 47.
8. *Kant's Political Writings*, p. 46.
9. I. Kant (1965) *Metaphysical Elements of Justice*, New York: Bobbs-Merrill, pp. 123–4.
10. Cf. S. Bok (1990) *A Strategy for Peace*, New York: Random House, p. 48.
11. *Kant's Political Writings*, pp. 93–6.
12. *Kant's Political Philosophy*, p. 200.
13. *Kant's Political Writings*, pp. 99–105.
14. *Kant's Political Philosophy*, p. 254.
15. *Metaphysical Elements of Justice*, p. 124; *Kant's Political Writings*, p. 171.
16. *Kant's Political Philosophy*, p. 260.
17. Cf. H. Williams (1987) 'Politics and philosophy in Kant and Hegel', in S. Priest (ed.) *Hegel's Critique of Kant*, Oxford: Oxford University Press, pp. 195–205.

Further reading

Bourke, J. (1942) 'Kant's doctrine of perpetual peace', *Philosophy* **17**: pp. 324–33.

Friedrich, C.J. (1948) *Inevitable Peace*, Cambridge, Mass: Harvard University Press.

Gallie, W.B. (1978) *Philosophers of War and Peace*, Cambridge: Cambridge University Press.

Gallie, W.B. (1979) 'Wanted: a philosophy of international relations', *Political Studies* **27**: 484–92.

Galston, W.A. (1975) *Kant and the Problem of History*, Chicago, Ill: Chicago University Press.

Hemleben, S.J. (1943) *Plans for Peace through Six Centuries*, Chicago, Ill: Chicago University Press.

Kant, I. (1963) *Kant on History* (ed. L.W. Beck), New York: Bobbs-Merrill.

Kant, I. (1977) *Kant's Political Writings* (ed. H. Reiss), Cambridge: Cambridge University Press.

Kant, I. (1989) *Kant's Selections* (ed. L.W. Beck), London: Macmillan.

Kemp, J. (1968) *The Philosophy of Kant*, Oxford: Oxford University Press.

Schwarz, W. (1962) 'Kant's philosophy of law and international peace', *Philosophy and Phenomenological Research* **23**: 71–80.

Shell, S.M. (1980) *The Rights of Reason*, Toronto: Toronto University Press.

Waltz, K.N. (1967) 'Kant, liberalism and war', *American Political Science Review* **56**: 331–42.

Williams, H. (1983) *Kant's Political Philosophy*, Oxford: Basil Blackwell; New York: St Martin's Press.

9 | HEGEL: THE MARCH OF WORLD HISTORY

Georg Wilhelm Friedrich Hegel was born in Stuttgart in 1770. The son of a civil servant, he was educated in Stuttgart and then at a seminary in Tübingen. Contemporaries of Hegel at the seminary were the poet Hölderlin and the philosopher Schelling. Hegel grew up at a momentous time. The events in France gripped his imagination and he is reputed to have planted a tree of liberty with his friends in Tübingen to celebrate the fall of the Bastille. Before becoming a university teacher at Jena in 1800 Hegel was a private tutor, first in Bern and then in Frankfurt. Some of his earliest philosophical writings date from this period.

Hegel is a compendious and most systematic philosopher. In taking his first philosophy post at Jena in 1800 he joined his friend Schelling, who expounded a system of absolute idealism. Hegel joined with enthusiasm the post-Kantian movement in German philosophy. Hegel saw in philosophy the key to the problems of everyday life and politics. By the time he became a professional philosopher he had come to the conclusion that politics on its own could not provide human salvation. The French Revolution failed to fulfil his earlier expectations. Life could be lived to the full only through the means of philosophy.

During the course of an eventful academic and philosophical career Hegel produced a comprehensive philosophical system. It is doubtful if any philosopher nowadays would attempt such a gigantic feat.

Hegel began his system with the publication of the *Phenomenology of Spirit* at Jena in 1807. (Reputedly he wrote the final paragraphs of the book to the sound of gunshots at the battle of Jena in 1806, won by Napoleon.) Hegel completed his philosophical system first in Nuremberg and then Heidelberg where he produced his *Science of Logic* (in two volumes) and the *Encyclopaedia of the Philosophical Sciences* (three volumes) and finally in Berlin, where he published the *Philosophy of Right* in 1821. The most accessible of his works is possibly the *Encyclopaedia*, particularly the first and third volumes on *Logic* and the *Philosophy of Spirit* respectively. Here the bare bones of his extraordinary system are presented. Hegel further developed his ideas in lectures on the *Philosophy of Fine Art*, the *Philosophy of History* and the *Philosophy of Religion*. Testament to his great productiveness is his work on the *History of Philosophy*. These lectures, along with those on art and religion, were published by his pupils after his death in 1831. Even the most popular editions of Hegel's *Collected Works* run to at least twenty volumes.

Hegel's political and international theory grows out of his extremely rich and diverse philosophical system. His political theory is outlined in its most comprehensive form in the *Philosophy of Right*. The central theme of Hegel's philosophical system is spirit or *Geist*. By this Hegel does not simply mean the human spirit nor the divine spirit. Spirit for him appears to represent a combination of the human, social and the divine. Hegel attempts to synthesize Christianity and philosophy. He sees the world as the product of *spirit*, and world history – in keeping with this – as the product of world spirit (*Weltgeist*).

At first sight the world appears as the other of the human mind as nature or a non-human artefact, but the philosophy of nature shows for Hegel that the world is at root intellectual, since it conforms to scientific laws which can be given to us by spirit. Spirit is present both now and in the past. History is the process of the external development of spirit and the internal development of spirit, which is charted in the history of philosophy. The object of political theory is to show the intellectual and spiritual nature of public and state life.

Hegel has often been attacked for his idealization of state life. Opinion in Britain and the United States has turned against him in this century at the time of the two world wars. He is accused of expounding an uncritical acceptance of the present social and political structures. He is identified with Prussianism since the state in which he lived from 1818 was Prussia and he was employed as Professor of Philosophy in Berlin from that time as a semi-official state philosopher. Close examination of the *Philosophy of Right* and the circumstances surrounding its publication does not bear out the claim that Hegel advocated a form of state idolatory. Not only is the *Philosophy of Right* in many respects critical of the conventional state of Hegel's day but also he ends up advocating a form of constitutional monarchy which runs counter to the arrangements of Prussia at the time.[1]

Hegel was a figure of the Enlightenment. He firmly believed in the power of reason. The purpose of philosophy in his view was to demonstrate the rationality inherent in things. So in his political theory he attempts to outline the sense and function of the political institutions and interstate relations of his day. For Hegel what is real is for that very reason rational.

That political institutions are in being and function implies for him a rationale. In this sense Hegel is very much like Aristotle who saw existing institutions as natural and therefore fulfilling a purpose.

The domestic scene – civil society

Contrary to the received impression Hegel's initial focus in the *Philosophy of Right* is the isolated human will, rather than the state. Hegel begins with the isolated individual in order to show how, step by step, intercourse with others is necessary, and fulfilment is born only from a rounded social and public life. In a sense Hegel's isolated human will is representative of humankind's condition in the state of nature. For Hegel the isolated will finds itself in a condition of abstract right. The rights it insists on, such as the satisfaction of desire, the ownership of property and personal liberty have an air of unreality about them taken on their own. They make sense and are realized only in the context of first civil society and then the state.

Hegel's description of civil society represents one of his major contributions to political theory. The concept of civil society is also of considerable importance to international relations. One of the key demands of the leaders of eastern European states in being freed from communism was for the establishment of 'civil societies' within their states. Hegel derives the term from Scottish political economy. By civil society Hegel means a sphere which is separate (yet related to) from the power of the state and the internal calculations of the individual. Classes belong to civil society but the family, individuality, personality and property do not. Civil society is what makes possible individual freedom in a concrete sense. Individuality outside civil society tends to selfishness and a civil society dominated by the state leads to the demise of individual freedom. In a sense the modern phenomenon of totalitarianism arises from civil society (as Hegel understands it) being extinguished.

In essence Hegel sees civil society as the sphere of the satisfaction of our material needs. We might now see it as, in the broadest sense, the economic sphere. In civil society we give expression to our individuality. Here we satisfy our needs: for pleasure, income, work and culture. At first sight in the market economy this leads to the most remarkable blending and compatibility of interests. As Adam Smith points out, each in pursuing private ends helps to bring about the public good. In rivalry and competition with each other, individuals in civil society add to the sum of the common wealth. There seems to be a kind of hidden hand operating which brings harmony to these outwardly competitive relations.

But this is not the end of the story for Hegel. He is not an uncritical exponent of the market. The spontaneous arrangements of civil society do not, in his view, wholly suffice to keep a check on conflict. Indeed as well as increased and beneficial wealth there are untoward consequences of the competition of civil society. First, there is no automatic balance between the interests of consumers and producers. Safeguards have to be introduced to ensure that the goods sold are of the quality required.[2] Second, the wealth produced is not evenly distributed. Wealth for one seems always to imply poverty for the other individual at the opposite pole in society. For Hegel civil society (or the capitalist economic system) can never be rich enough. In creating riches for some it tends also to impoverish others.[3]

Some of these form a penurious rabble who may well put civil society under threat. This rabble has for Hegel to be minimized and its disruptive effects countered. Hegel has no ready answer for the poverty engendered by capitalism. In artificially making the poor better off, you may undermine the spirit of independence which makes civil society what it is. High unemployment benefits do not therefore deal with the problem. Providing work through the public authorities also does not necessarily solve the problem, since unemployment is caused in the first place by a lack of demand for commodities. Public works projects seem to be the best prospect in Hegel's eyes, but even here society might not feel that in times of recession it could afford to pay for them. It would be misleading therefore to regard Hegel as a Keynesian, who favours increased government expenditure as a means of overcoming recession, before his time.

Hegel's conclusion seems to be that there is an unavoidable element of instability in modern civil society. This instability feeds through into the international system. Sovereignty in relations with other states is unavoidably linked with sovereignty at home. The state has to assert itself in both spheres. Hegel attributes such instability to continuous technical change and the continuous change in consumer needs related to it. For Hegel civil society wrests the individual from home, kith, clan and locality. The mobility of labour and the freedom it creates is a product of the market economy. Thus the state must provide some welfare benefits to replace those former means of social support provided by the family and locality. But the state cannot take responsibility for the individual. The price of independence is possible failure. Cyclical fluctuations in trade also seem difficult to avoid, and one way of dealing with the problem of lack of demand for manufactured goods is to expand overseas. Hegel saw this as a solution Britain had in his time adopted. Colonization provided an opportunity to establish new markets abroad and also a means of acquiring valuable raw materials. Hegel could not contemplate any alternative type of economy to the market system since he feels that the personality of the individual depends too much upon the ownership of private property. Individuality would wither where the economy comes under the control of the state: for Hegel a state communist system would be bound to fail.

Yet the state has to be present and active for civil society to prosper. No civil society can wholly live with itself. Civil society requires a power higher than itself to guide it through its more difficult times. In order to avoid damaging conflicts between consumers and producers the state has to set standards (eg quality of product, conditions of production) to ensure that one side does not take advantage over the other. The worst collisions between the market and those who are dependent upon it have to be overcome.

Equally there has to be a state in order that laws can be modified and revised. Hegel regards civil society as being perfectly capable of administering the law but not of making it. Corporations (both public and private) provide for Hegel an important mediating force between the state and civil society. Corporations do not banish the conflicts which arise among the conflicting parties in civil society but they do aggregate them and thus make them easier to manage. They provide institutions and leaders with which the legislature and executive can deal. Indeed Hegel thinks that corporations should be represented in the legislature or parliament.

Hegel favours a direct form of representation which reflects the functional divisions of civil society. Emphasis should be placed on representation since he does not think the ordinary citizen qualified actually to direct the affairs of the state. Unlike Kant, Hegel would keep the ordinary individual and the philosopher entirely out of international politics. The main purpose of representation for Hegel is to alert the state to the problems of the market economy and civil society. The advantage he sees with functional representation is that as well as raising the problems of civil society the representatives can transmit the government's response to the public in the most effective way.

Hegel thinks the state should be elevated above everyday life. It should possess a majesty which it is wise not to call into question.[4] To reflect the awe in which the state should be held Hegel believes the crown (monarch) should be involved both in the executive and the legislature. The monarch should have the final say as the head of the executive (after taking advice) and should also have its representatives set alongside other representatives in the legislature. To back up the power of the monarch Hegel would like a second chamber where hereditary landed interests are represented. Some features of the Hegelian state are very close to the actual characteristics of the British constitution at that time.

Hegel departs from liberal belief in not wanting to see the separation of powers under the constitution. Executive, legislature and judiciary should come under the crown. Seemingly the model of the American revolution did not appeal to Hegel. In his opinion such a division can set the state at war with itself, thus undermining its majesty. Hegel sees individuals as possessing rights, but these are rights in the context of a state. There are strictly speaking no natural rights or cosmopolitan right. Hegel cannot envisage a supreme court defending the rights of individuals on the basis of conceptions of human rights in general. Although Hegel is not seemingly against a written constitution it appears that he thinks the existing government should be an authority on its interpretation. He could not go along with an appeal to a written constitution which would undermine a new practice derived by the state. Hegel shows a preference for states based upon tradition rather than ones established on the basis of rights.

It seems that Hegel elevates the state to such an extent because of his concerns about sovereignty and the rule of law. Given the conflicts which are an unavoidable part of civil society and international life it seems inconceivable to Hegel that a nation can hold together as a whole unless the sovereignty of the current ruler is sustained. The state has to rise above the conflicts of the business, cultural and private worlds. Its activities can be criticized but its legitimacy should never be threatened.

In this apparent panic about the consequences of the pursuit of private interest and social conflict Hegel seems to have done himself and the cause of liberalism a great deal of harm. Putting the majesty of the state before the rights of the people tends to undermine the very rule of law which Hegel so cherishes. Settled sovereignty is necessary to preserve the law, but the object of the preservation of law (as I see it) is to defend the rights of individuals from arbitrary arrest, from assault and intimidation, loss of their possessions, etc. As the power of the state is raised above the press of private interest there comes a point at which individual rights begin to get undermined.

A Napoleonic-style state, where the executive, legislature and judiciary is monopolized by one power, can become a danger to itself. Hegel fails to accept the consequences of the fallibility of human government. In order that his monarch can sustain its claim to sovereignty he has to be entirely beyond reproach. Hegel seems to have no concept of an individual fulfilling the *role* of sovereign. Hegel in fact expressly rejects the notion of popular sovereignty. It may well be true that the masses who riot in the street cannot be seen as worthy of sovereignty, but unless citizens see that they are in some respects collectively sovereign no sense of political responsibility can develop.

The great difficulty with Hegel's rigid division between civil society and state is that as ordinary individuals we are not called upon to consider our wider civic responsibilities. Rampant individualism may make us into strangers to each other and strangers in relation to the state which we inhabit. Somehow social and political power has to permeate the mass without social unity being destroyed. Parliamentary representation has to be real rather than nominal. The people should legislate through their representatives and the executive should be answerable to the people (as well as separate from the legislature).

Hegel probably achieved his stated aim in his account of the modern state. He gave a representative view of what he found before him. The political system of the United States diverges from his ideal but might not at the time be regarded as wholly beyond his scope. The modern European state –

possibly as a consequence of the French Revolution – has been irresponsible in relation to its citizens. We have attributed an infallibility to our sovereign authorities which has never been borne out in practice. We have both expected too much and too little of our rulers. The modern state highjacks the sovereignty of the people and Hegel justifies this.

The international arena

Hegel's theory of international relations is greatly influenced by his view of history. For Hegel history is the product of spirit (*Geist*).[5] Spirit is not the same as, but incorporates, the Hebrew and Christian ideas of God. Spirit is Hegel's expression for the ideality of experience. Like Plato, Hegel believed that the essence of reality was thought. In this way the history of the world is contained in spirit. We know spirit only from its past: the next steps in the progress of the world are known to spirit alone.

For Hegel there are three types of historical writing. These are original history, reflective history and philosophical history. In the first type of history the author's spirit, 'and that of the actions he narrates, is one and the same'. Thucidydes may be an example of this kind of historian. In reflective history the 'working up of the historical material is the main point'.[6] Here historians develop their own point of view, attempting to put together a story. However, in philosophical history the focus is upon the totality of human events. Here it is suggested that 'the history of the world ... presents us with a rational process'.[7]

Hegel cannot separate philosophical history from the Christian religion. He remarks 'we must not imagine God to be too weak to exercise his wisdom on the grand scale'.[8] Because they are not conversant with the Christian tradition 'the orientals have not attained the knowledge that spirit – man as such – is free' and because they do not know this, they are not free. They know only that one is free, and that one is 'therefore only a despot; not a free man'.[9] In contrast the Greeks knew only that some are free, not humankind as such.

Spirit goes through four stages in the process of its development. Beginning with the oriental world whose principle is complete oneness: spirit moves on to the Greek, Roman and, finally, Germanic worlds. For Hegel this is the history of the unfolding of human freedom. In the Greek world the seeds of human freedom are sown in the political life of the city-state; this freedom is developed in a one-sided way with the Roman Empire and brought to its maturity in the Christian, and particularly Protestant, ethos of modern Europe. Hegel thought that the constitutional monarchies of his day represented the highest form of freedom.

In sum, Hegel thought that 'the history of the world is none other than the progress of the consciousness of freedom; a progress whose development according to the necessity of its nature, it is our business to investigate'.[10] We should not spare ourselves from the most realistic view of history,

> but even regarding history as the slaughter-bench at which the happiness of peoples, the wisdom of states, and the virtue of individuals has been sacrificed – the question involuntarily arises – to what principle, to what final aim these enormous sacrifices have been offered.[11]

History and the development of states should not be seen as subject wholly to external laws ordained by spirit. Indeed 'nothing . . . happens, nothing is accomplished, unless the individuals concerned, seek their own satisfaction in the issue'.[12] Individuals have their special needs and concerns through which spirit evinces itself. Like Machiavelli, Hegel sees individual action as playing a role in history: 'we may affirm absolutely that nothing great in the world has been accomplished without passion'.[13] Hegel coins the phrase 'world-historical individual' to refer those people who successfully act with audacity and passion in history. Such world-historical individuals are different from ordinary people in that they may act against the norms and laws of their state. Political philosophy applies to us as ordinary citizens within a given state. Great leaders however act upon a different world-historical stage. They challenge conventional norms and social expectations and differ from the ordinary person who does the same in that they do so successfully.

'World-historical men – heroes of an epoch – must, therefore, be recognised as its clear-sighted ones; their deeds, their words are the best of that time.' None the less, 'great men have formed purposes to satisfy themselves not others'.[14] To act in such a world-historical pattern is not a comfortable existence. It may be with such individuals 'when their object is attained they fall off like empty hulks from the kernel'.[15] Hegel criticizes the idea that great men seek to do what they do merely from the most narrow subjective motives. The idea, for instance, that Alexander of Macedon partly subdued Greece and then Asia because he was possessed by a morbid craving for conquest is very shallow. These are the ideas of those who are mere bystanders in the historical process. 'No man is a hero to his valet-de-chambre', and this is not 'because the former is no hero, but because the latter is a valet'.[16] There is an arbitrary side to the role of such an individual: 'so mighty a form must trample down many an innocent flower – crush to pieces many an object in its path'.[17] This cruelty may not be the product of malice but simply the consequence of the achievement of great ends.

Just as Kant had seen history and world politics leading to consequences unwilled by any of the participants so Hegel thinks that there may operate in history a similar force which he calls the cunning of reason (*List der Vernunft*). This cunning of reason 'sets the passions to work for itself, while that which develops its existence through such impulsion pays the penalty and suffers loss'.[18] In working itself out, an idea may have to sacrifice and abandon the individual. Hegel sees this not as the fault of the ideal itself but as the outcome of the limitations of individuals. History may well go through some regretful periods as a consequence of the envy, greed and ambition of individuals. Indeed, so grandiose is Hegel's view of the onward march of history that he is prepared to state 'that as a general rule, individuals come under the category of means to an ulterior end'.[19] This is a view that we might find morally reprehensible. Yet he does stress that the subjective side must have its place. Morality, ethics and religion have a role to play in the onward march of spirit. The individual is not wholly a means within the larger historical process. Not only do individuals in the act of realizing historical aims 'make it the occasion of satisfying personal desires, whose purport is diverse from that aim – but they share in that ideal aim itself'. By being at one with the ideal aim individuals can play their part in history. It has always to be recognized though that 'the claim of the world spirit rises above all special claims'.[20]

The prime object to be realized by the means of world history is the 'ethical whole, the State, which is that form of reality in which the individual has and enjoys his freedom'.[21] For Hegel whatever spiritual or ethical reality we possess we possess through the state. Since when 'the subjective will of man submits to laws – the contradiction between liberty and necessity vanishes'.[22] In obeying the laws of their state, individuals are submitting themselves to spirit, since law for Hegel is the way in which spirit realizes itself in an objective way in society.

In humans in contrast to nature there is found an impulse for perfectibility. This lies behind the progress which may be discerned in world politics. Changes in nature, no matter how varied and exotic they might be 'exhibit only a perpetually self-repeating cycle'. We might legitimately say of the physical world that 'there is nothing new under the sun'.[23] This is not so with human life. The human species develops. But this development does not take place in a harmonious way. In history, 'spirit is at war with itself; it has to overcome itself as its most formidable obstacle'.[24] 'The realization of its idea is mediated by consciousness and will.'

History exhibits a curious dialectic:

In actual existence progress appears as an advancing from the imperfect to the more perfect; but the former must not be understood abstractly or only the imperfect, but as something which involves the very opposite of itself – the so called perfect as germ or impulse. . . . Thus the imperfect, in that it implies its opposite, is a contradiction, which certainly exists, but which is continually annulled and solved; the instinctive movement – the inherent impulse in the life of the soul – to break through the rind of mere nature, sense, and that which is alien to it, and to attain to the light of consciousness, ie to itself.[25]

Yet the levels which 'spirit seems to have left behind it, it still possesses in the depths of its present'.[26]

Interstate relations fall into the ebb and flow of the development of world history. Hegel sees an overall pattern of progress, but a great deal of misery, confusion and anguish lie between humankind and the achievement of this goal. There is, it seems, no direct upward path to progress. For Hegel it would be folly to outline a plan for perpetual peace. The future course of history is not for mere humans to plan. Just as foolish would be an attempt to bring about a federation of states bound by the objective of attaining peace. This misunderstands world society which moves forward as much through discord as harmony.

There is a negative side to international politics. Hegel thinks we have to live with this negative side. We cannot look to world politics for justice, happiness or lasting glory. Many things happen in an arbitrary way. States are won and lost, constitutions are created and destroyed. Borders are violated, countries are torn in half, prosperity is destroyed. Peace is never fully gained. One war is concluded only for another to be set in hand. A Hegelian would not be surprised that the Cold War and the war in Indo-China grew directly from the victories of the allies in the Second World War. At the level of appearance relations among states are arbitrary and often cruel.

Hegel appears to believe in stressing the difficulties and problems of international life. External relations are 'on the largest scale a maelstrom of external contingency and the inner particularly of passions, private interests and selfish ends, abilities and virtues, vices, force and wrong'.[27] Those contradictions have a deeper meaning. The continual conflicts of international life are the way in which the guiding thread of human history – *Weltgeist*/world-spirit – evinces itself. For Hegel there is something mystical in human life. A purpose comes to the fore which is not the purpose of any of those individuals involved. Thus is somewhat similar, it seems, to Machiavelli's *fortuna* without the possibility of exercising *virtu*. At the level of international society we can leave it to spirit to see that everything is well. Providence lies in the background although we cannot be certain what direction it will take.

Because there is an underlying purpose to the negativity (or the simple unpleasantness of war) of international society Hegel takes an unusual attitude to war. War is not, he thinks, to be regarded as absolute evil which has to be avoided at all costs. It was, he seems to suggest, inherent in the international society of his day. There was even an ethical side to war. A war brings into question the very existence of a state. Citizens who are normally engrossed solely in their own interests realize the value of the security they enjoy. 'War is the state of affairs which deals in earnest with the variety of temporal goods and concerns'.[28] In seeing that they might be expendable, citizens work to restore the prosperity of their state.

Hegel takes the Greek view that life within the state is the highest form of life. Doing your public duty – obeying your state – is the most commendable form of ethics. He is not impressed by a form of morality which looks solely to the individual conscience in deciding what is right: the individual moral standpoint should for Hegel be superseded by a socially oriented ethic. War brings out the ethical necessity for the state. No form of ethical life is possible without its protection. States/rulers may sometimes use this fear positively by engaging in war to dampen down domestic unrest. A successful war, Hegel recognizes, can 'consolidate the power of the state at home'.[29] Some commentators, in keeping with Hegel's comments, have regarded the seizure of the Falkland Islands by Argentina in 1983 as an attempt by the ruling junta to divert attention away from failed domestic policies.

Hegel is prepared to grant the existence of international law. However, it is as an 'ought to be': it exists not as something positive but only in so far as states are prepared to grant its validity. It is always possible that a dispute may be settled by international law, but it is not necessary. International law seems to draw attention to the precarious nature of relations among states. International law requires, for instance, that peace treaties should be kept. But whether in fact this is so depends upon the sovereign states themselves. It seems equally to be a precept of international law that if a state cannot obtain satisfaction through making representations and arbitration then it has always the recourse to war: 'If states disagree and their particular wills cannot be harmonised, the matter can only be settled by war'.[30]

Hegel thinks that we should not be shocked by this. The upward progress of the human race towards freedom necessitates disharmony. In their conflicts with each other states often bring out what is best in them. The higher principle ultimately triumphs over the lower. Hegel takes this optimistic view because he believes that the course of the world is ultimately in the hands of world-spirit. One state can come to embody for a time the highest stage of human life, but it may in the future be surpassed by another state. Growth, decline and fall are part of the pageant of human history. No nation stays on top for ever – or does it? Hegel thought the European state embodied the highest ideal for his time. Has it now been surpassed by states of the east and west?

Hegel says of the USA in his *Philosophy of History* that it

is the land of the future where in the ages that lie before us, the burden of the history of the world shall reveal itself – perhaps in a contest between North and South America. It is a land of desire for all those who are weary of the historical lumber-room of old Europe. . . . It is for America to abandon the ground on which hitherto the history of the world has developed.[31]

To be set against this, though, is Hegel's equally strongly expressed view that 'the history of the world travels from east to west, for Europe is absolutely the end of history, Asia the beginning'.[32]

Notes

1. S. Avineri (1972) *Hegel's Theory of the Modern State*, Cambridge: Cambridge University Press, pp. 176–83.
2. Hegel (1969) *Philosophy of Right*, trans. M. Knox, Oxford: Oxford University Press, p. 147, para. 236.
3. *Philosophy of Right*, p. 150, para. 245.
4. Cf. M. Levin and H. Williams (1887) 'Inherited power and popular representation: a tension in Hegel's political theory', *Political Studies* 35: 105–15.
5. P. Singer (1983) *Hegel*, Oxford: Oxford University Press, ch. 1.
6. Hegel (1956) *Philosophy of History*, New York: Dover, p. 2.
7. *Philosophy of History*, p. 9.
8. *Philosophy of History*, p. 15.
9. *Philosophy of History*, p. 18. See also Avineri, *Hegel's Theory of the Modern State*, p. 224.
10. *Philosophy of History*, p. 19.
11. *Philosophy of History*, p. 21.
12. *Philosophy of History*, p. 23.
13. *Philosophy of History*, p. 26.
14. *Philosophy of History*, p. 30.
15. *Philosophy of History*, p. 32.
16. *Philosophy of History*, p. 32.
17. *Philosophy of History*, p. 32.
18. *Philosophy of History*, p. 33.
19. *Philosophy of History*, p. 33.
20. *Philosophy of History*, p. 37.
21. *Philosophy of History*, p. 38.
22. *Philosophy of History*, p. 39.
23. *Philosophy of History*, p. 54.
24. *Philosophy of History*, p. 55.
25. *Philosophy of History*, p. 57.
26. *Philosophy of History*, p. 79.
27. *Philosophy of Right*, p. 215, para. 340.
28. *Philosophy of Right*, p. 210, para. 324. See also S.B. Smith (1989) *Hegel's Critique of Liberalism*, Chicago, Ill: Chicago University Press, pp. 156–64.
29. *Philosophy of Right*, p. 210, para. 324.
30. *Philosophy of Right*, p. 214, para. 334.
31. *Philosophy of History*, pp. 86–7.
32. *Philosophy of History*, p. 103. Avineri, *Hegel's Theory of the Modern State*, pp. 236–8.

Further reading

Avineri, S. (1972) *Hegel's Theory of the Modern State*, Cambridge: Cambridge University Press.
Cullen, B. (1979) *Hegel's Social and Political Thought*, London and Dublin: Gill and Macmillan.

Fackenheim, E.L. (1967) *The Religious Dimension in Hegel's Thought*, Chicago, Ill: University of Chicago Press.

Hegel, G.W.F. (1969) *Philosophy of Right*, trans. M. Knox, Oxford: Oxford University Press.

Hegel, G.W.F. (1956) *Philosophy of History*, New York: Dover.

Kaufman, W. (ed.) (1970) *Hegel's Political Philosophy*, New York: Atherton.

Marcuse, H. (1969) *Reason and Revolution*, London: Routledge.

Pelczynski, Z.A. (1973) *Problems and Perspectives in Hegel's Political Philosophy*, Cambridge: Cambridge University Press.

Plamenatz, J. (1963) *Man and Society*, vol. 2, London: Longmans.

Plant, R. (1983) *Hegel*, Oxford: Basil Blackwell.

Smith, C. (1965) 'Hegel and war', *Journal of the History of Ideas* **26**: 282–5.

Taylor, C. (1979) *Hegel and Modern Society*, Cambridge: Cambridge University Press.

Wilkins, B.T. (1974) *Hegel's Philosophy of History*, Ithaca, NY: Cornell University Press.

Williams, H. (1989) *Hegel, Heraclitus and Marx's Dialectic*, London: Harvester; New York: St Martin's Press.

10 | CLAUSEWITZ: THE STRATEGIC DIMENSION

Carl von Clausewitz was born the fourth son of Friedrich Gabriel Clausewitz in Burg near Magdeburg, Prussia, in 1780. His father was a retired lieutenant who held a minor post in the Prussian internal revenue service. Carl Clausewitz first encountered war in 1793 as a 13-year-old infantry ensign. He served in the Rhine campaigns of 1793 and 1794 against the French, receiving his commission at the siege of Mainz in 1793.

In 1795 Prussia withdrew from the war. In 1801 Clausewitz was sent to the war academy school in Berlin for young officers. The director of this school was Scharnhorst, who was to have a great influence on Clausewitz's life from then on. From Berlin Clausewitz became an aide-de-camp to Prince August of Prussia. War broke out once again with France in 1806. Clausewitz was wounded and taken prisoner with his commander by the French. They were held in France and then Switzerland until 1808.[1] The Prussians were catastrophically defeated by Napoleon in this war. Napoleon entered Berlin and desecrated many of Prussia's national monuments. This defeat led to a considerable rethinking of Prussian military strategy and practice. Scharnhorst played a considerable part in this reconsideration and brought Clausewitz into his group. A number of progressive political reforms also took place under von Stein and Hardenburg, leading to a greater civil participation in the government of the country.

Perhaps the most painful experience of Clausewitz's military career took place in 1812, when Prussia signed a treaty involving collaboration with the French. Clausewitz resigned his commission and spoke out against what he took to be the cowardly action of his colleagues. He was driven to write a short speech in defence of his position: 'I declare and assert to the world and to future generations that I consider the false wisdom which aims at avoiding danger to be the most pernicious result of fear and anxiety.'[2] For him 'a people must never value anything higher than the dignity and freedom of its existence'.[3] He regarded the treaty with France as nothing short of a national capitulation. And he is moved to state his position on international affairs: 'In my judgement the most important political rules are: never relax vigilance; expect nothing from the magnanimity of others; never abandon a purpose until it has become impossible, beyond doubt to attain it; hold the honour of the state as sacred.'[4]

The risk that Clausewitz took in leaving the service of the Prussian king in 1812 and joining the Russian army appears to have paid off. Although thoroughly disliked by some of his fellow-officers for apparently betraying the national cause, Clausewitz was ultimately to do his beloved state a far greater service. Through his work and like-minded individuals in the Prussian army, Prussia was able to emerge on the victorious side when Napoleon was defeated.[5] For a while Clausewitz was able to serve with the commander-in-chief of the Prussian army in Mainz. This surely must have represented a total reverse of his experience in the Rhineland in the 1790s. But his reforming and independent thinking led to his withdrawal from the commander-in-chief's office to the tranquility of Berlin. In Berlin he was made administrative head of the War Academy. Seemingly this was not a particularly influential post; the major fruit of these years in Berlin was the writing of Clausewitz's major theoretical work *On War*. Clausewitz died in the cholera epidemic of 1831 (the same epidemic that brought Hegel's death).

Kantian or Hegelian?

The impression that I gained of Clausewitz in reading *On War* was that of a most humane and disciplined person. The book makes no attempts to glorify its topic. At one point he speaks about paying heed to our *feelings* at points of crisis when rational judgements seem to have failed. Clausewitz appears to mean by our feelings an inner sense of self, possibly rooted in the desire for self-preservation. Emotion in most ordinary circumstances is to be shunned but in moments of great danger (and, possibly, despair) it would be folly to overlook the signals they give us. Even the most rational of strategies has its breaking point.[6] Strategic and military thinking has to take this into account.

Further evidence of Clausewitz's apparent humanity is his own military and public career. In his career he appears to have been motivated by a desire to get things right. This seems not simply to have been the zealous sense of duty to the state one might expect from a Prussian officer, but rather a desire also for professionalism in the career one has chosen – a civil standpoint which has far wider implications. Clausewitz saw military life as a job which might be done well, poorly or not at all. He set himself a task apparently of trying to devise rules which might allow one to excel at the vocation of military leadership. He saw these rules as being interwoven with politics and relations among states. Clausewitz is the military equivalent of Machiavelli.

Yet Clausewitz may plausibly have been a Kantian in the political theory he adopts. There is evidence that he was taught in his youth by the Kantian Kieswetter. Furthermore we have the evidence of Clausewitz's own writings, which appear to be heavily Kantian in tone. We can envisage Clausewitz taking with enthusiasm to Kant's invocation (following Frederick the Great) in his essay on Enlightenment 'to argue as much as you like but obey!'7 In his political writings Kant made it clear that he expected military activity would be subordinate to political activity. This is one reason why in his essay on *Perpetual Peace* Kant prefers a citizens' army to a solely professional army. He feels that if the main occupations of soldiers are civilian rather than military this will lead to a greater circumspection in the use of force. Although Clausewitz seems not to share Kant's views about the transformation of the military, Clausewitz is none the less emphatic that military action should be seen primarily as an extension of political action.

In contrast to this Kantian view of Clausewitz is Azar Gat's interpretation of Clausewitz as a convinced Hegelian. As with Kant it is difficult to find direct evidence of Clausewitz's reading of Hegel, but there is possibly sufficient circumstantial evidence to demonstrate that Clausewitz knew Hegel's works well. In a fascinating passage Gat speaks of Clausewitz's possible use of Hegelian dialectic in outlining his military strategy.8 And it may well be that the opposites which play such a prominent part in Clausewitz's presentation, such as that between real and absolute war, and the notion of war as a contradictory human activity, draw upon Hegel's thinking.

But Gat also suggests there is an affinity between Hegel's political theory and Clausewitz's position. Like Hegel, Clausewitz's political theory is centred upon the nation-state. Gat feels that Clausewitz must have been deeply impressed by Hegel's *Philosophy of Right* published in 1821.9 Clausewitz tends to regard the state as an ethical totality in the manner of Hegel. And the thesis which Hegel puts forward in the *Philosophy of Right* is that the state is the foundation and the realization of our freedom.

There is also a striking affinity, as Gat notes, between Hegel's ideas on war and international relations and those expressed by Clausewitz. Clausewitz shares with Hegel the belief in the apparent insignificance of international law and also argues that war can have beneficial effects upon the civilian population. Gat cites from Clausewitz this passage to demonstrate the connection:

> Today practically no means other than war will educate people in this spirit of boldness. Nothing else will counteract the softness and the

desire for ease which debase the people in times of growing prosperity and increasing trade. A people and nation can hope for a strong position in the world only if national character and familiarity with war fortify each other by a continual interaction.[10]

In taking such a Hegelian perspective Clausewitz comes across as a strong patriot and political realist.

It seems clear that Clausewitz would have nothing to do with Kant's cosmopolitanism which to Clausewitz might seem weak and excessively liberal-minded. To prosper, a state must be prepared to conflict with others. But it is not sure that Clausewitz can be claimed entirely for the Hegelian camp. As Paret notes Clausewitz's experience with the Prussian state during the Napoleonic wars seems to have led to some distancing between the military theorist and his native society. Paret intimates that there is possibly a maturing towards a greater objectivism in Clausewitz's outlook, towards the view that the state was a central fact of political life but not a suitable object to which to accord our entire affections. Paret speaks interestingly of a period of disappointment with the Prussian state which was followed by a 'process of psychological separation' 'which eventually enabled him to think of Prussia with nearly the same objectivity that he applied in his judgement of any major power'. Strikingly Paret concludes that 'for Clausewitz the Prussian state ceased to be what it continued to be for Hegel: the realization of an ethical idea. Instead, he regarded it as a historical reality whose first duty is to maintain itself.'[11] Paret finally sees Clausewitz's political ideals as representing ultimately a return to Machiavelli 'who emphasized the primacy of the structure and mechanics of power'.[12]

War as a duel

Clausewitz brought out the political nature of war: war is a means to an end, not an end in itself. The desire for glory may play a part in the fighting of a war, but Clausewitz thinks it would be wrong for it to enter into the motives of a military commander. If military commanders are to be successful they have to approach their tasks in a professional way. The demands of the intellect should come before the demands of personal vanity. No war should be prolonged for more than is necessary to achieve the aim of defeating the enemy. This is why it may be necessary for both military and humanitarian reasons to use the maximum of force, which will bring about the swiftest victory.

Kant saw a convergence occurring between truth, rationality and morality. In doing the right thing for Kant we are not only following the dictates of our conscience but also doing what reason and truth oblige us to. There is an extraordinary rigorism in the Kantian view. It seems a person following a Kantian ethic can enjoy an element of certainty about the rightness of their action. I think there needs to be caution about making any absolute claims in ethics and politics. Clausewitz appears, however, to be intensely Kantian in his approach, expressing, perhaps, as much his and Kant's common Prussian culture as Clausewitz's familiarity with Kant's writings. Clausewitz demands of the military genius that he should always have regard to the inner dictates of his conscience. The military leader should demonstrate 'an intellect that, even in the darkest hour, retains some glimmerings of the inner light which leads to truth; and, second, the courage to follow this faint light wherever it may lead'.[13]

The successful military leader then is a person who can act dispassionately without ignoring the impact of passion and emotion upon individuals and who will participate in war because it is a necessary human activity. Although war involves the utmost brutality and suffering the military leader should strive at all times to be above it. All is lost if the commander is dragged down into the brutish world 'where danger is shunned and shame is unknown'.[14] The commander should not lose sight of human dignity 'the noblest pride and deepest need of all: the urge to act rationally at all times'.[15] In typically Kantian fashion Clausewitz does not think to ask how widely and deeply this need is felt.

Clausewitz and international politics

International society can be viewed from a variety of divergent perspectives. It can be viewed from the standpoint of all the participants involved. All the actors – states, politicians and peoples – can be seen as taking part in one drama which has as its plot perhaps the betterment – or the downfall – of the human race. It can be viewed from the standpoint of some of the participants involved say, perhaps, the English-speaking peoples, the African people or the international working class. Here the object is to denote the career of one group and probably to advance it. International society can also be viewed from the standpoint of one of the participants involved – one state, nation or group of political leaders. An approach which lends itself to this point of view is the *strategic* approach. It is in this sphere that Clausewitz makes his contribution to the study of international society.

In writing *On War* Clausewitz took for granted that states were the main actors in international society and that it was legitimate for the state to use the military means at its disposal to achieve its objectives. Clausewitz leaves to others the question as to whether the present arrangements of international society are the best. His standpoint is the military one: given the present nature of international society how best can his state (Prussia) achieve its goals. This is a day-to-day realist perspective on peoples and states. Peoples and states unavoidably quarrel among themselves. They use armed forces to prosecute those quarrels. How should those armed forces be arranged and employed to gain the best advantage in the dangerous world of international politics?

War, for Clausewitz, 'is nothing but a duel on a larger scale'.[16] The object is to get the better of the opponent. It may be that in a war a state may have more than one enemy, but this then can be treated as a series of duels. War is, of course, fought for victory but the object of victory is 'to compel our enemy to do our will'. In these duels in international society Clausewitz sees force as playing the major part there are 'certain self-imposed, imperceptible limitations' like international law and custom but they are 'scarcely worth mentioning'.[17]

In employing war as a means of advancing our ends in international society a leader should learn to put kindness to one side. (As he says in his earlier speech on his beliefs: 'expect nothing from the magnanimity of others').[18] In Clausewitz's view, the worst mistakes in war are made from kindness.[19] If in war it is known that one side will desist from certain acts of cruelty and another will not – say, the large-scale bombing of civilian populations, as occurred in Dresden and Hiroshima – the side that is prepared to act most cruelly has the advantage. Not to be at a disadvantage requires the participant to recognize that 'war is an act of force, and there is no logical limit to the application of that force'.[20] Whatever level of force one opponent employs has to be matched by the other or else the duel will be lost.

The purpose of war is to render an enemy incapable of being an enemy. The enemy has to be disarmed. To disarm your enemy you must be in a position to coerce him. And coercion can be made possible if you put your enemy in a position that is even more unpleasant and distressing than the sacrifice you call on him to make. The key thing is that the prospects for your opponents in persisting with their action will be worse than if they give it up.

Anyone undertaking a war enters the realm of chance. Any theory of war cannot be intellectually complete. As M.I. Handel puts it, 'to Clausewitz war was a messy affair that could not be reduced to a set of lessons and laws.'[21] There is no strategy that will always succeed. Military commanders have to live by their wits as much as by their intelligence. Because gambling plays such a large part in war, the quality required of a successful leader is, above all, courage. But courage without good sense is a danger. Even in daring there has for Clausewitz to 'be method and caution'.

Certainty cannot be brought to the conduct of war by war itself. War for Clausewitz falls firmly under the control of politics.[22] 'War is not merely an act of policy but a true political instrument, a continuation of political intercourse, carried on with other means'. Although from the strategic standpoint war may appear to be an end in itself, and the ethos of war the most laudable one, the overall perspective into which war falls should not be lost sight of. 'The political object is the goal, war is the means of reaching it, and means can never be considered in isolation from their purposes'.[23]

The clear message for international politics is that the strategic dimension should not get the upper hand. Political consideration and military consideration have to be weighed together with political considerations being given precedence. War is 'a paradoxical territory – composed of violence, hatred and enmity . . . of the play of chance and probability within which the creature spirit is free to roam; and of its element of subordination, as an instrument of policy, which makes it subject to reason alone'.[24] Clausewitz regards the underlying spirit of war as emanating from the people. The passion with which a war is fought depends on the character-istics and situation of the nation prosecuting it. Courage and talent are supplied by the armed forces themselves. But policy, to which the whole is subordinate, is solely the business of the government.

Friction in war

Experience is crucial in war. One cannot conceive of all the difficulties faced by a commander unless you have been involved in an engagement with the enemy: 'Countless minor incidents – combine to lower the general level of performance, so one always falls short of the intended goal'.[25] It is like having to do things when you are tired. After three late nights the performance of the simplest task – tying one's laces, for instance – becomes very difficult. This effect in war Clausewitz calls *friction*. *Friction* is what distinguishes *real* war from *war* on paper. All the difficulties of war can be overcome by iron will. However, this employment of an iron will takes it out on the machine. Even the most capable leader needs rest and relaxation. Continued stress will tend to undermine the capability of the most determined person.

Under the friction of war unpredictable factors such as the weather can become an absolute menace. When fog descends it may wholly destroy an advance or, on the other hand, lead to avoiding an agonizing defeat. Each war is 'an uncharted sea, full of reefs'.[26] Clausewitz argues that friction cannot be fully defined. Indeed the wisest military commanders are not those who dwell on its effects. Rather, the best commanders are those who are acquainted with the effects of friction and know how to avoid it.

> Action in war is like movement in a resistant element. Just as the simplest and most natural of movements, walking, cannot easily be performed in water, so in a war it is difficult for normal efforts to achieve even moderate results.[27]

Absolute and limited war

Clausewitz does not advance the distinction in quite this way. For him it is, initially at least, a distinction between absolute and *real* war. An element of confusion belongs to the prosecution of most wars. Although the 'natural aim of military operations is the enemy's overthrow' and hostilities cannot be said to have ended until one or other 'side is finally defeated'. Much occurs in practice to dull this precise picture. Since 'most wars are like a flaring-up of mutual rage',[28] the exact course and outcome of the event is difficult to discern. Wars may not be fought with the aim of mutual destruction. The destruction of the enemy represents but one extreme point on the spectrum of possible aims. The clarity of aims may well be lost and means may become as important as ends. Clausewitz puts it well when he says

> logic comes to a stop in this labyrinth; and those men who habitually act, both in great and minor affairs, on particular dominating impressions or feelings rather than according to strict logic, are hardly aware of the confused, inconsistent, and ambiguous situation in which they find themselves.[29]

For Clausewitz the most striking exponent of absolute war is Napoleon. 'After the short prelude of the French Revolution, Bonaparte brought it [the war] swiftly to that point'.[30] Napoleon's wars were fought without respite. Napoleon could not settle until he emerged finally as the total victor or, as happened in the end, the vanquished.

In general though, since so many variables are involved in war – emotion, good or bad luck, a huge interplay of possibilities – it necessarily follows that 'war can be a matter of degree'. And as war can be fought both in an absolute sense and in a real sense outlined here, there are two concepts of success.

In absolute war it is only final victory that counts. Contrasting with this extreme view is another view 'no less extreme – which holds that war consists of separate successes each unrelated to the next.'[31] It is taken that the outcome of earlier conflicts have no effect upon the later. Conflict begins always from scratch. But Clausewitz thinks that even in the second type of war the first idea cannot be discarded entirely. He is prepared to recognize the significance of the second kind of limited war – politics may so hem in military action that no other conception may for a time be possible. Sometimes it is 'legitimate to pursue minor advantages for their own sake and leave the future to itself'.[32] However, from the military perspective the concept of absolute war takes precedence for Clausewitz. In the modern era in particular absolute war with its devasting power is unquestionably with us. Yet in prosecuting an absolute war it is worthwhile bearing in mind that 'small things always depend on great ones, unimportant on important, accidentals on essentials'.[33]

On the whole the object of a limited war is defence. For the most part it involves 'holding one's own until things take a better turn'.[34] But there are two kinds of limited war that is an 'offensive war with limited aims and defensive war'.[35] We may try to turn defence into attack. We may set ourselves a less significant target and seek to overcome the enemy locally. In a limited war alliance might well play a more significant part since we cannot rely on our own forces alone to overwhelm the enemy. But for Clausewitz it is important to bear in mind one country may support another's cause, but will never take it so seriously as it takes its own.[36]

Real war

I think in looking at this question Clausewitz takes a strongly Hegelian dialectical standpoint. In considering military strategy it is usual to regard war as the opposite of normal human intercourse. War is seen as the exception to the ordinary ordered relations of states, individuals and societies. In Clausewitz's opinion it is in our nature to regard war as an aberration. This is something that 'no philosophy can resolve'.[37] In truth, war and ordinary human intercourse are mutually dependent qualities. The two opposites are united. And 'this unity lies in the concept that war is only a branch of political activity; that is in no sense autonomous'.[38] Thus real war (as opposed to absolute war which is characterized by continuous tension and hostility) is closer to a mixture of outright hostilities and peace. In real war neither the fighting nor the tranquillity quite gain the upper hand. Clausewitz may therefore be suggesting that most 'real wars' are wars of attrition where the attrition takes on both a military and moral form.

Whatever is the answer to this question Clausewitz's famous dictum that 'war is simply a continuation of political intercourse, with the addition of other means'[39] appears to derive from his view that war and peace are closer together than is ordinarily imagined. War cannot be divorced from political life. Were they intellectually to be separated 'we are left with something pointless and devoid of sense'.[40]

In Clausewitz's view, the military and political leader would be wise to see the dependence of one on the other:

> We will find that war does not advance relentlessly toward the absolute, as theory would demand. Being incomplete and self-contradictory, it cannot follow its own laws, but has to be treated as part of some other whole; the name of which is policy.[41]

There is a warning here then to military leaders not to forget their allegiance to their political masters and the suggestion that 'a certain grasp of military affairs is vital for those in charge of general policy'.[42] The military dimension is a significant aspect of relations among states, but it is not the sole or the most significant aspect. The strategic viewpoint influences, but is secondary to the political viewpoint.

The evidence is, in conclusion, that Clausewitz is not an internationalist. Cosmopolitanism he links with liberal weakness. Each state should first of all look to itself. If states have patriotic citizens and are well run this is to the advantage of civilization in general. In enhancing its national security a state enhances its prestige and so gives self-confidence to its citizens. Clausewitz was used to the Napoleonic state. Under Napoleon, France had become the leading European power and this was achieved through the full mobilization of the people for the cause of the nation. Clausewitz saw this characteristic lacking among the German people. He saw little wrong in the German people showing a similar concern for the standing of their nation.

This stress on national security and patriotism may from time to time lead to the outbreak of war. For Clausewitz this is only to be expected. It is part of the healthy working of the system. Like Hegel, Clausewitz was impressed by the capacity of war to re-awaken in people a respect for their state and with it a heightened awareness of citizenship. In terms of international society this is a doctrine of continuous tension. Clausewitz is combatitive without being inhumane. Through conflict human powers are stimulated and developed. But the history of the German people seems to suggest that there are limitations to the applicability of this view of international society. A state that constantly seeks prestige through military power may find the power ranged against it too great for it to survive. Also with the advent of nuclear weapons other limits are placed upon the uses of military power. Military power springs back on itself. The weapons of destruction become so powerful that they may well lead to self-destruction. It is possible that large sections of international society have outgrown the condition Clausewitz outlines. Patriotism and competition among states have to take on a non-military form for them to remain valuable traits in world society.

Finally, one of Clausewitz's most significant distinctions is the one between absolute and real war, which leads to one other interesting point in his writing, namely his view that war is policy pursued by other means. Clausewitz was perceptive enough to see that under most conditions it was extremely difficult for a war to be pursued to a complete and final victory. This is the goal of absolute war, but it is by its nature almost unattainable. In the first place, any military defeat, however total, can be viewed by the vanquished as a new starting-point. A state can accept defeat in the short run only to prepare for a later victory. In the second place, all wars are hemmed in by the underlying political factors which have led to it. If those factors change military victory may not be necessary. The result is that in real wars politics always interferes with the military strategy. Clausewitz thinks that this is rightly so. War must be subordinate to political policy since it is only one means of pursuing political goals. Thus Clausewitz's doctrine of real or limited war (in my view) places war in a proper perspective. In the circumstances of his time Clausewitz saw the preparation for war and their prosecution as part of international society. This was because political cirumstances dictated such preparedness. But Clausewitz's approach leaves open the possibility, that should political circumstances change, then the attitude of political leaders towards war might also change. As Sissela Bok has tried to show, Clausewitz's strategic approach is not wholly incompatible with the pursuit of peace.[43]

Notes

1. M. Howard (1983) *Clausewitz*, Oxford: Past Masters, pp. 8–9.
2. 'I believe and profess', in Clausewitz (1965) *War, Politics and Power*, ed. E.M. Collins, Chicago, Ill: Gateway, p. 301.
3. 'I believe and profess', p. 301.
4. 'I believe and profess', p. 304.
5. Howard, *Clausewitz*, p. 9.
6. 'In the dreadful presence of suffering and danger, emotion can easily overwhelm intellectual conviction, and in this psychological fog it is so hard to form clear and complete insights that changes of view become more understandable and excusable. Action can never be based on anything firmer than instinct, a sensing of the truth'. Clausewitz (1976) *On War*, Princeton, NJ: Princeton University Press, p. 108.
7. H.S. Reiss (ed.) (1977) *Kant's Political Writings*, Cambridge: Cambridge University Press, p. 55.
8. A. Gat (1989) *A History of Military Thought*, Oxford: Oxford University Press.
9. *A History of Military Thought*, p. 241.
10. *A History of Military Thought*, p. 244; *On War*, p. 192.
11. *A History of Military Thought*, p. 438.
12. *A History of Military Thought*, p. 43.
13. *On War*, p. 102.
14. *On War*, p. 105.
15. *On War*, p. 106.
16. *On War*, p. 75.
17. *On War*, p. 75.
18. 'I believe and profess', p. 304.
19. *On War*, p. 75.
20. *On War*, p. 77.
21. M.I. Handel (1986) *Clausewitz and Modern Strategy*, London: Frank Cass.
22. *On War*, p. 87.
23. *On War*, p. 87.
24. *On War*, p. 89.
25. *On War*, p. 119.
26. *On War*, p. 120.
27. *On War*, p. 120.
28. *On War*, p. 579.
29. *On War*, p. 579.
20. *On War*, p. 580.
31. *On War*, p. 582.
32. *On War*, p. 583.
33. *On War*, p. 596.

34. *On War*, p. 601.
35. *On War*, p. 602.
36. *On War*, p. 603.
37. *On War*, p. 605.
38. *On War*, p. 605.
39. *On War*, p. 605.
40. *On War*, p. 605.
41. *On War*, p. 605.
42. *On War*, p. 605.
43. S. Bok (1990) *A Strategy for Peace*, New York: Random House, pp. 55-76.

Further reading

Aron, R. (1976) *Clausewitz*, London: Routledge.
Clausewitz, C. (1976) *On War*, Princeton, NJ: Princeton University Press.
Clausewitz, C. (1968) *On War*, Harmondsworth: Penguin.
Gat, A. (1989). 'Clausewitz's political and ethical world view', *Political Studies* **37**: 97-106.
Howard, M. (1965) *Theory and Practice of War*, London: Cassels.
Howard, M. (1983) *Clausewitz*, Oxford: Past Masters.
Paret, P. (1976) *Clausewitz and the State*, Oxford: Oxford University Press.
Paret, P. (ed.) (1986) *Makers of Modern Strategy*, Oxford: Oxford University Press.
Reynolds, C. (1978) 'Carl von Clausewitz and strategic theory', *British Journal of International Studies* **4**: 178-96.
Smith, H. 'The womb of war: Clausewitz and international politics', *Review of International Studies* **16**: 39-58.

11 | MARX: THE COLLAPSE OF INTERNATIONAL CAPITALISM

Karl Marx was born in Trier in 1818. Trier lies on the River Moselle near the present-day border between France and Germany. It is likely that Trier society in Marx's youth was drawn as much towards France as Germany. The memory of the French Revolution and the ascendancy of Napoleon was still fresh in people's minds. Marx began his academic career at Cologne University (1835–6) but after an eventful year his father decided to send him to Berlin. The University of Berlin was thought to provide a more sober academic context for the young Marx to pursue his studies. At Berlin Marx made the acquaintance of a number of radical thinkers, who formed a group called the Young Hegelians. German philosophy was still in the thralls of Hegel's extraordinary system and to make a mark youthful philosophers had to take a critical stand in relation to it. It was the circle of the young Left Hegelians that Marx joined in Berlin.

A notable member of this group was Ludwig Feuerbach: his materialist humanism greatly influenced Marx. Marx was particularly struck by Feuerbach's handling of the notion of alienation. Feuerbach used the idea to criticize the Christian religion. He particularly wanted to undermine the Christian idea of another, more perfect, world beyond this life. Marx, however, found other uses for the concept of alienation and in this he was greatly influenced by Friedrich Engels, whose acquaintance he made in Paris in 1843. Engels introduced Marx to the study of political economy, a subject developed to its most advanced form by the British (particularly the Scottish). The intellectual power of Marx's thinking is drawn from its fusion of critical German philosophy with the empiricist tradition of political economy. It is also often argued that Marx's system was completed by a strong infusion of French revolutionary thinking – particularly socialist.

Marx's vision of national and international society rests, as it does with the other thinkers we have considered, on his notion of human nature. Marx's conception of human nature is a particularly fluid one. It cannot be said with any conviction that his conception of human nature is fully developed even within his own writings.[1] It appears that Marx begins in his early writings with a view of the human being as a being of pressing, objective natural needs. Human individuals are never complete in themselves. We need food to sustain ourselves, shelter from the elements and the company of others to form a society. Marx then would find much to commend in Hobbes's antagonistic account of our natural condition. But there is reason to believe that Marx might be sceptical about the entire vision of natural humankind that Hobbes presents. Marx stresses co-operative production as much as he does individual rivalry and conflict. It is labour which makes humans into what they are.

Thus, on one view Marx can be regarded as thinking that the nature of humans is a continually unfolding story. Because he sees our natures are formed by the circumstances encountered in our existence it is difficult to provide one final picture. As we are creatures with natural needs our first problem is to subdue nature. We shape ourselves in this continually evolving struggle with nature. Our relationship to nature is a productive one and it changes in accordance with the methods and means of production we have at our disposal. Technology then helps alter and shape how we are. Our tools not only are extensions of our personalities but also mould and shape how we are.

Economy and world society

As opposed to Hegel's account of the division of human history into various stages, which Hegel broadly categorizes along cultural lines (Oriental, Greek, Roman and Germanic periods), Marx suggests a division more based upon modes of production. Marx called these periods the Asiatic, the slave, the feudal and the capitalistic modes of production. The Asiatic mode of production was a form which went hand in hand with despotism since there was but one landlord and co-ordinator of economic activity and that was the state. With slavery, which characterized Ancient Greek and Roman society, the individual producer was owned by a master. Under feudalism the direct producers came under the control of the lords through their ownership of the land, and under capitalism the worker comes under the control of the employer through the employer's control over capital. Marx felt that different types of human society and intersocietal relations corresponded with these methods of production. As he puts it in the *German Ideology*: 'the relations of different nations among themselves depend upon the extent to which each has developed its productive forces, the division of labour and internal intercourse'.[2]

Marx's and Engels's theory of international relations might be gleaned from their essay on *German Ideology*, the *Communist Manifesto* and the Preface to the *Introduction to a Critique of Political Economy* published by Marx in 1859. Each of these works gives an outline of their *historical materialism*. The best-known summary is given in the *Preface of 1859* where Marx argues that the impetus for historical change comes from the economic basis of society. By the economic basis of society Marx means its forces and relations of production. As the economy of a society develops so then its ideological superstructure alters. Ideological supertructure is the phrase Marx uses to describe all the forms of thought and culture associated with society at a certain stage of its development. As he puts it,

> in the social production of their existence, men inevitably enter into definite relations, which are independent of their will, namely relations of production appropriate to a given stage in the development of their material forces of production. The totality of these relations of production constitutes the economic structure of society, the real foundation on which arises a legal and political super-structure.... The mode of production of material life conditions the general process of social, political and intellectual life.[3]

The political organization of society is largely part of this ideological superstructure which is altered as the economy changes. For instance, the middle class came to power in Britain primarily because of the growth of the market economy. Its political power was a product of its economic supremacy and not vice versa.

Marx's and Engels's view of international society would broadly follow the same pattern. The key influence upon relations among states would be their economic relations. For instance, Britain now finds itself in a somewhat subordinate position to the United States in the world, according to this view, because it lags behind the United States in the size of its economy and the speed of its development. Following this view, the rising stars of the international system would be those states such as Japan and South Korea whose economies were developing most rapidly and were introducing the most advanced technologies. To bring about a reasonable harmony among the states of the world Marxists would attach a reasonable amount of importance to establishing just economic relations among states. The debtor status of large numbers of Third World countries would, in their view, stand in the way of achieving fairly harmonious north–south relations in the world.

In the *Communist Manifesto* Marx and Engels see the progress of world history largely in economic terms. Class struggle they see as a primary motivation to conflict in society. For them all recorded history is a history of class struggle. Class relations arise in their view through one group in society gaining a monopoly over the means of production (economy). In modern society it is the conflict between the capitalist class and the working class that takes centre stage. They see this both as a national struggle and an international struggle. The *Manifesto* closes with the words 'working men of all countries unite'.[4] Marx sought to give practical effect to this by establishing an International Working Men's Association in the 1860s.

Marx's political theory is therefore inherently an international theory. Marx sees politics not from the perspective of one national state but from the perspective of a progressive view of history with the international working class as its agent. Marx and Engels's fundamental historical premiss is that all previously documented societies have been class societies. What defines class for Marx is an individual's relation to the means of production. By 'means of production' it seems Marx intends to summarize all those economic factors which make possible our social existence. What has happened up to now in history is that those factors have, as Marx sees it, been controlled by one group at the expense of all other members of society. According to this view the ruling class in any society is the class that owns the means of production. Historically there have been differences in the kind and extent of the ownership of the economic basis of society. In Ancient Greece the ruling group owned not only the means of production but also the producers themselves. Classical Greece was a prosperous society built upon slavery. In feudal society the ruling class exercised its control over the population through its ownership of the land. The loyalty of serfs to their masters went with the land on which they eked out their existence. In feudal society (still a feature of European life for a large part of this century) the land does not belong to the serf, the serf belongs to the land. As Marx sees it, under the capitalist system, despite all appearances to the contrary, class rule remains because one group, the bourgeoisie, owns the means of production in factories, land, offices and shops with which it controls the daily lives of the large majority.

The main advantage of a class society from the point of view of the ruling group is that it gives rise to a surplus of wealth which can be shared out among members of the group. The subordinate class does not merely produce sufficient for itself, it is obliged by the dominant class to produce enough to support it as well. Indeed the more efficient the class system the greater economic surplus it gives rise to. A characteristic of a class society is, as Marx understands it, that the social wealth is in private hands. This we can see is a characteristic of capitalist society where large industrial and financial corporations dominate the economy.

According to Marx the capitalist class comes on to the scene with the development of worldwide trade and the colonization of America, Africa and India. The expansion of trade and the exploitation of new countries allowed great fortunes to be amassed which was the basis of the first great industrial undertakings. Marx regarded the English potentate and adventurer Clive of India as an example of this early type of capitalist accumulator.

Once industry takes the place of small-scale craft manufacture the development of capitalism goes ahead in leaps and bounds. More and more products are manufactured following detailed industrial methods. More and more capitalists appeared as new ways were discovered of producing familiar and necessary objects cheaply. Side by side with their increasing economic importance the political significance of the capitalists grows. In the beginning capitalists were prepared to establish their businesses under the protection of feudal governments. But these traditional governments try to protect economic and social rules which are inimicable to the development of capitalism. The tax imposed upon salt in pre-revolutionary France is an example of this kind of restriction. The free movement of goods and labour is a necessary feature of capitalist society. Such traditional stifling regulations have to be removed to strengthen the growth of capitalism. By 1848 the bourgeoisie had gradually, Marx and Engels say, 'conquered for itself, in the modern representative state, exclusive political sway'. As a consequence 'the executive of the modern state is but a committee for managing the common affairs of the whole bourgeoisie'.[5]

Marx and Engels saw the bourgeoisie as an enormously innovative class. In their view the class survived by continually revolutionizing the means of production. Capitalists improved production techniques to make better products and then to stay ahead of their rivals. Capitalists also were essentially expansive in their attitude to the world. They required continually expanding markets for their goods, they were also continually hunting for even-more plentiful supplies of raw materials. These forces drove them overseas. In the remoter parts of the world they discovered new markets and new sources of raw materials. Capitalists, according to Marx and Engels, 'nestle and settle everywhere'.[6] A world culture develops in the wake of capitalist expansion. As a result of each nation industrializing the whole world gradually becomes more urbanized. Populations are concentrated in larger and larger cities. As nations become more centralized so the world as a whole follows. Each individual is continually made conscious of his or her common interest with the rest of humanity. What happens in Moscow affects intimately what happens on the New York stock exchange. In short, capitalism creates international politics.

But, of course, a further part of Marx's thesis is that the growth of the influence of the bourgeoisie does not go unopposed. As the bourgeoisie develops and grows stronger as a worldwide class, the class over which it rules grows stronger and more powerful as well. The working class becomes a political force to be reckoned with as well. Workers forge their own national and international organizations. First, these are organizations of defence. Through these organizations there is an attempt made to improve the immediate material conditions of the working class. But the lessons drawn from the organization of trade unions is then applied to the political sphere. Political parties of the working class are born. These working-class political parties lead the struggle between capitalists and workers on a national and international level.

The working class has to create its own separate political and economic organizations because its interests, Marx claims, are diametrically opposed to those of the capitalist class. The constant revolutionizing of the mode of production which is part and parcel of a capitalist economy does not go ahead without its difficulties and problems. Changes in production are a result of competition between firms. One firm survives by driving others out of business. Each business has to face the possibility of a downturn in market conditions. Although the market is a mechanism for matching supply with demand it does so often with great unevenness. There is no absolute certainty that all the goods produced will be consumed, just as there is no certainty that all consumer demands can be met. Indeed it is often so that capitalist society suffers from crises unheard of in former societies, what Marx and Engels call 'crises of overproduction'. 'Society suddenly finds itself put back into a state of momentary barbarism; it appears as if a famine, a universal war of devastation had cut off the supply of every means of subsistence; industry and commerce seem to be destroyed'.[7] For them such crises are a symptom of what they describe as barbarism within civilization. They feel that with such crises capitalism tends to undermine itself.

The role of the working class as Marx and Engels see it is to usher in – both nationally and internationally – a new form of society. The hallmark of the new society would be social ownership of industry and commerce with production according to a common plan. Marx and Engels regard the workers as forming a revolutionary class. Members of the class have, in their view, everything to gain from the overthrow of existing society. The struggle for the liberation of the working class has, in their view, a unique feature not shared by any previous revolutionary movement. All such movements in the past had been movements of minorities. They resulted in the emancipation of one group of people in society who formed the new ruling class. But the working class forms the vast majority in modern society and can emancipate itself only by getting rid of class rule altogether.

As class rule rests upon the private ownership of the means of production a working-class revolution would abolish all ownership in the means of production. For the first time, as Marx and Engels see it, men and women would organize the economy on a planned basis, instead, as now happens, of the economy managing them behind their backs. Since the majority was in charge there would be no possibility of another group taking surplus production away from the producers themselves. The surplus production of society would go towards meeting social needs, many of which would be the needs of producers themselves.

The paradox about Marx and Engels's view of social revolution is that they think the dictatorship of the working class will lay the basis for the ending of all class conflicts. Class antagonisms exist, they argue, because one group – a minority – controls the economy and uses this control for its own benefit. However, the working-class movement which establishes the dictatorship of the proletariat is the movement of the great majority. Marx and Engels envisage international harmony coming about through the producers controlling the world economy. They imply that present-day conflicts in international society are largely caused by capitalist states quarrelling among themselves.

Marx regards the working class not so much a class of modern society but more as a class existing outside that society. Workers are somehow expelled from respectable society. This leads him to the argument that because the workers have no proper home within their societies they will not possess nationalist sentiments. Workers' attachment is not to their country but to humanity in general.[8] This has turned out to be an unfortunate generalization. In practice workers have often turned out to be as nationalistic or even more nationalistic than members of other social classes. The thesis is that if capitalism is international then the workers have to organize internationally to overcome it. In doing this they lose their nationalistic standpoints. Empirically then there appears not to be a great deal of evidence to corroborate Marx's belief that in removing capitalism workers may be led to international solidarity. Although there have been a number of heroic attempts to live up to the ideal, such as the formation of the International Brigade during the Spanish Civil War.

Marx applies this historical materialist view of the world most directly to international society in the theory of colonization that he advances in *Capital*.[9] Marx implies that political policy and legislation have unavoidably to vary between mother-country and colony because of the differences in economic relations. Employees in a colonized society were at greater freedom to choose their mode of employment. There was unsettled land at their disposal. Thus, to ensure an adequate workforce Britain was, for example, obliged to limit the supply of land in North America. But this artificial imposition of barriers from the mother-country was regarded as unjust by large sections of the colonial population. This quite naturally led to a desire for greater independence. Like Hegel, Marx also saw large-scale emigration to colonial countries as a product of the surplus population of the mother country which encouraged a larger working population than it could itself support.

Imperialism

International theory comes into its own in Marxism with the work of Lenin on *Imperialism* (1916). Lenin was not the first Marxist to turn his attention to the problem of Imperialism. The Austrian socialist Rudolf Hilferding, who was later to be a minister of finance in Germany in the Weimar period, discussed the problem in detail in his book on *Finance Capital* (1910). Hilferding saw finance capital as bringing an entirely new dimension into the world economy. Antagonism existed among capitalist states because they were competing for each other's markets. On the one hand this led to the imposition of tariffs to protect their home markets while on the other it led to a drive for greater expansion overseas. As Hilferding puts it:

> whereas on one side the generalization of the protective tariff system tends increasingly to divide the world market into distinct economic territories of nations states, on the other side the development towards finance capital enhances the importance of the size of the economic territory.[10]

Economies of scale in production made it extremely attractive to have large and numerous markets. In their external policy states were therefore torn between protection and free trade. Economically weak states might well favour protection to develop their industries, but at the same time they would stand to profit by the free trade policies of other nations.

The growth in size of firms and their increase in profits leads to an amassing of financial capital. This spare financial capital needs an outlet and it finds this outlet in the 'export of capital'. For 'the export of capital accelerates the opening up of foreign countries and promotes the maximum development of their productive forces. At the same time it increases domestic production, which has to supply the commodities that are exported abroad as capital'.[11] Colonization therefore marches hand in hand with the export of capital.

According to Hilferding the export of capital brings about a change of political behaviour in the metropolitan countries. When trade was the main avenue of contact with these overseas territories the metropolitan countries were more or less indifferent towards the modes of government which existed. Now with export capital at stake and the land, railways, harbours, mines, and other fixed installations, they bring in their train far more sophisticated methods of supervision are necessary. The exporting country needs to create its own colonial state. As a result within the dependent state 'the old social relations are completely revolutionized, the age-old bondage to the soil of the "nations without a history" is disrupted and they are swept into the capitalist maelstrom'.[12]

The process of development and change does not, however, stop there. Capitalism awakens in the native population the desire for its own freedom. They begin to want their own state in which they can seek their own wealth and advance their own culture. But this 'independence movement threatens European capital precisely at its most valuable and promising areas of exploitation, and to an increasing extent it can only maintain its domination by continually expanding its means of coercion'.[13] Thus, the bloody battles of decolonization of the twentieth century may have been implicit in the process of colonization itself. The strong colonial state was creating those very forces, such as a prosperous indigenous middle class, which were to undermine itself.

Hilferding places particular stress on the increase in tension among advanced capitalist state brought about by the export of capital and colonization. He believes that imperialism leads to a decline in significance of humanitarian ideals in public life: 'in place of the idea of humanity there emerges a glorification of the greatness and power of the state'.[14] In its early days the bourgeois state had been the focus for national loyalties, a way of drawing one culture together. Other nations were to acknowledge the right to create and safeguard their own states. With the export of capital and colonization this egalitarian ideal is dispensed with. 'The ideal now is to secure for one's own nation the domination of the world, an aspiration which is as unbounded as the capitalist lust for profit from which it springs'.[15] Hilferding interestingly attaches this international quest for power with the rise of racist ideology. Through racism an apparently scientific justification can be put forward for the subjection of one group by another. What is a consequence of the economic expansion of capital can then be passed off as a natural phenomenon.

Lenin wrote his short pamphlet on *Imperialism* in Zurich in the spring of 1916. Written in the midst of the turmoil of the first world war it reflects a low point in the development of international socialism. As K.N. Waltz has pointed out, the internationalist ideals of Marxian socialism appeared to suffer a terminal blow with the support shown for the war by the various national parties of organized labour.[16] Against this vision of a broken ideal Lenin was trying to revive the cause of international socialism. As with many prominent Russian socialist leaders at the time he felt that the cause of Russian working class might be revived only through a more general European upheaval. Thus for Lenin imperialism appeared as an enemy against which he might rally socialists everywhere. He sought to transform the seeming defeat of socialism represented by the general war into an advantage.

Lenin draws on the work of Hilferding and the English liberal writer J.A. Hobson in giving his account of imperialism. Lenin's thinking may have been given a strongly dialectical turn by the extensive reading of Hegel he undertook at the time. Lenin agrees with Hilferding that capitalist imperialism is an outgrowth of the economic system built up by financial capital, however he is more apocalyptic than Hilferding about the consequences of the 'cancer' of imperialism.

Lenin connects imperialism with the size of modern industry. Marx had argued that with capitalism there is a tendency toward the centralization and concentration of production. The onward march of the society in his view led to the undermining of small-scale producers. The German socialist Bernstein disputed this view in a series of well-known articles in *Die Neue*

Zeit, the theoretical journal of the German party, suggesting that small-scale industry was just as vibrant as ever.[17] Lenin, true to his revolutionary goal, weighs in on the side of the opponents of Bernstein in arguing that monopoly was becoming the prevailing pattern. While there always seems room for the new small-scale producer under capitalism it seems also that a long-term trend is the one that Lenin denotes. Nowadays we see all around us in the west an economic world dominated by large corporate giants who compete among themselves for world business. The larger the corporation and the more competitive the environment the larger it seems the market has to be to absorb the output. Each corporation has to think on an international scale to survive.

Finance capital also enters into our everyday lives in a dramatic way. Banks are quite often used by a large number of individuals and groups simply as a place to store and save money. But we are now also used to the more active side of bank activity in initiating loans either for private purposes of consumption or for corporate and individual purposes of investment. In controlling and giving access to funds for investment banks are potentially able to wield a great deal of power. The decisions of bankers can spell life or death to corporations. Banks may not be able wholly to specify the use to which a loan is put, but through the rate of interest stipulated it can specify the rate of return. Modern industry requires investment on a very large scale to sustain its level of activity. Competition often compels firms to undertake larger and larger investments to keep in touch with the latest technology in the industry. The scale of production increases enormously at the same time as the market expands.

In the Preface to the French and German editions of *Imperialism: the Highest Stage of Capitalism* Lenin argues that 'as this pamphlet shows, capitalism has now singled out a handful of exceptionally rich and powerful states which plunder the whole world simply by "clipping coupons"'. Capital exports yield an income of 'eight to ten thousand million francs per annum'.[18] Instead of a vibrant participatory economy you now have in the metropolitan centres a rentier society. Decadence and parasitism are features of these metropolitan societies. Wealth instead of being attached to production is now attached to idleness. The model of the successful person in these imperial societies is the person who does the least labour but enjoys the highest income. But this decadence and complacency spreads to other classes. Out 'of such enormous superprofits... it is possible to bribe the labour leaders and the upper stratum of the labour aristocracy'.[19] The better-off sections of the working class are drawn into the ways of the rentier economy. It is this section of the working class whom Lenin blames for the success of militarism and the outbreak of war in the main European countries in 1914.' This stratum of workers-turned-bourgeoisie, or the labour aristocracy, who are quite comfortable in their mode of life... is the principal prop of the Second International, and in our days, the principal social (not military) prop of the bourgeoisie'.[20] The failure of international socialism to capture the masses of Europe in 1914 – despite the apparent strength of socialist parties in countries like Germany and Britain – was not according to Lenin due to any weakness in the Marxist theory of social development but was rather due to the fallibility and corruptibility of labour leaders who should have known better. In short, the tactics that the Second International and the individual socialist parties employed in combatting war fever and nationalism were wrong.

A particular feature of capitalism that leads to imperialism is, according to Lenin, the concentration of production and monopolies. The larger the company the bigger the market it requires in order to sell its goods. Within branches of industry and commerce in one country like Britain or France one company gets to dominate. In the first instance this dominance may not take on the form of complete monopoly, but as time progresses this may well be established. Monopoly at home intensifies the competition abroad. Companies come to regard parts of the world market as being their own. For instance one company may dominate the Latin American market for steel. But its domination is never safe. Steel companies from other capitalist states will seek to break this domination.

A means of overcoming this damaging competition is through the establishment of cartels among the biggest producers. These cartels – which are co-operative organizations of companies in a given line of industry – may operate to stabilize the market at both a national and international level. A present-day example of a cartel is the Organization of Petroleum Exporting Countries (OPEC), which brought about a major economic crisis in the early 1970s by withholding supplies to push up prices.

But Lenin is not convinced that cartels can act to stabilize markets and production.

> The statement that cartels can abolish crises is a fable spread by bourgeois economists who at all costs desire to place capitalism in a favourable light. On the contrary, the monopoly created in certain branches of industry increases and the anarchy inherent in capital production *as a whole*.[21]

Reforming socialists like Eduard Bernstein had argued that the existence of cartels had considerably altered the competitive nature of capitalist production. Bernstein was even to imply that because of such changes as this a revolutionary transformation of capitalism, as foreseen by Marx, was no longer necessary. Lenin wanted to avoid this conclusion, perhaps feeling that in his native Russia it was only revolution that would undermine Tsarism. Lenin also felt it was a complacent conclusion for a socialist to draw. Lenin had no desire simply to stand back and observe capitalism transform itself. Left to itself capitalist imperialism might well destroy civilization.

Lenin's view is that the imperialist stage of capitalism cannot be sustained for long. He sees capitalism as being in a cul-de-sac with no further means of evolution. Imperialism therefore represents capitalism in its death throes. Possibly Lenin was driven to this image by the carnage that he saw going on all around him in the First World War. No doubt for a relatively detached spectator something may have appeared to be radically amiss with the European state system in 1916.

Enormously aiding the centralization of production and distribution taking place in the main capitalist states was for Lenin the growth of the power of the banks. The original role of banks had been to accept deposits of money and to aid in the payment of creditors. In this capacity banks came to lend money to their established and credit-worthy customers. Under large-scale capitalism the lending activity of the banks increases out of all proportion:

> As banking develops and becomes concentrated in a number of establishments, the banks grow from modest middlemen into powerful monopolies having at their command almost the whole of money capital of all the capitalists and small businessmen and also the larger part of the means of production and sources of raw materials in any one country and in a number of countries.[22]

The banks come not only to oil the wheels of industry but also to initiate and end production. The large banks establish an enormous power over their customers. The larger the customer and consequently the greater the investor – both home and abroad – the more it can be in the power of the banks. For Lenin 'the result is ... the ever-growing merger or as N.I. Bukharin calls it, coalescence of bank and industrial capital'.[23] Capitalism is internationalized through the banks and the export of capital. Banks can transmit decisions and capital immediately from one part of the globe to the other. In the modern world they are an international power in their own right. Capitalism in a monopolistic form gives a world system. In essence it cannot be paralysed in one part without affecting everywhere else. Hence, Lenin concludes it can be defeated only by world revolution.

Lenin saw the European states not only becoming their own worst enemies but also creating opponents through their overseas expansion. If European capitalism was not going to decay from within it looked as though it was going to be undermined from without. The European states needed their overseas territories as markets and outlets for their export capital. They could not afford to lose them. But this is precisely what the movements for colonial independence were threatening to do: to detach the colony from the mother state.

Lenin's cataclysmic view was quite naturally connected with his own revolutionary purposes in Europe and, more particularly, Russia. He probably wanted to gain support among European socialists and intellectuals for his view that something could be done about the plight of Europe. In fighting to overthrow capitalism in Europe socialists were knocking upon an open door. But it seems Lenin had not reckoned with the adaptability of capitalism and its controllers. The very limits to capitalist expansion and survival that Lenin could discern were visible also to his opponents.

Lenin might have noted that not all capitalists states had followed the path of political expansion overseas. The amount of colonization undertaken by the United States, arguably already the most advanced capitalist state, was very small indeed. The United States appeared to be developing a different pattern of relationships with more backward nations: here the export of capital and the opening up of markets was taking place without annexation. Latin American has for the most part enjoyed an independent political relationship with the United States. Nationalist movements in Latin America have not then represented a direct threat to American dominance of the hemisphere. Indeed it might be argued that the best interest of the United States lies not in the subordination of the other state of Latin America, but in encouraging them to develop along the same lines as themselves. Successful international capitalists might see that it was in their own long-term interests to have a developed Third World.

With the benefit of hindsight we can see (which Lenin did not) that the social and political order of capitalism was not in a terminal condition. Indeed it might be unwise in general to regard societies in such an organic way. Societies may not follow the path of individual living things of coming into being, being and passing away. Societies seem, on the contrary, to exist through transformation. Lenin plays down the voluntarist side of human history and emphasizes the determinist side. Probably it is an error to regard the course of events as decided in advance – although this may provide us from time to time with reassurance. I find it more reassuring to believe that we cannot know with certainty what lies ahead, although we ourselves may well play a part in shaping the outcome.

Notes

1. N. Geras (1983) *Marx and Human Nature*, London: Verso.
2. L.D. Easton and K.H. Guddat (eds and trans.) (1967) *Writings of the Young Marx on Philosophy and Society*, New York: Anchor, p. 410.
3. Marx (1971) *Contribution to the Critique of Political Economy*, London: Lawrence & Wishart, pp. 20–1.
4. Marx and Engels (1968) *Selected Works in One Volume*, London: Lawrence & Wishart, p. 63.
5. *Selected Works*, p. 37.
6. *Selected Works*, p. 37.
7. *Selected Works*, p. 37.
8. *Selected Works*, p. 44.
9. Marx (1970) *Capital*, vol. 1, London: Lawrence & Wishart, pp. 765–75.

10. R. Hilferding (1985) *Finance Capital*, London: Routledge, p. 311.
11. *Finance Capital*, p. 314.
12. *Finance Capital*, p. 322.
13. *Finance Capital*, p. 322.
14. *Finance Capital*, p. 355.
15. *Finance Capital*, p. 335.
16. K.N. Waltz (1965) *Man, the State and War*, New York: Columbia University Press, pp. 126–58.
17. See E. Bernstein (1961) *Evolutionary Socialism*, New York: Schocken Books.
18. Lenin (1968) *Imperialism: The Highest Stage of Capitalism*, Moscow: Foreign Language Press, p. 12.
19. *Imperialism*, p. 12.
20. *Imperialism*, p. 12.
21. *Imperialism*, p. 26.
22. *Imperialism*, p. 28.
23. *Imperialism*, p. 41.

Further reading

Cohen, G. (1978) *Marx's Theory of History*, Oxford: Oxford University Press.
Conway, D. (1987) *A Farewell to Marx*, Harmondsworth: Penguin.
Elster, J. (1985) *Making Sense of Marx*, Cambridge: Cambridge University Press.
Hilferding, R. (1985) *Finance Capital*, London: Routledge.
Kemp, T. (1967) *Theories of Imperialism*, London: Dennis Dobson.
Kolakowski, L. (1978) *Main Currents of Marxism*, 3 vols, Oxford: Oxford University Press.
Lenin, V.I. (1968) *Imperialism*, Moscow: Foreign Languages Press.
McLellan, D. (1974) *Karl Marx: His Life and Thought*, London: Macmillan.
McLellan, D. (1979) *Marxism after Marx*, London: Macmillan.
McLellan, D. (ed.) (1988) *Marxism: Essential Writings*, Oxford: Oxford University Press.
Marx, K. and Engels, F. (1968) *Selected Works in One Volume*, London: Lawrence & Wishart.
Marx, K. (1971) *Contribution to the Critique of Political Economy*, London: Lawrence & Wishart.
Marx, K. (1970) *Capital*, vol. 1. London: Lawrence & Wishart.
Suchting, W. (1983) *Marx: An Introduction*, Brighton: Wheatsheaf.
Williams, H. (1988) *Concepts of Ideology*, Brighton: Wheatsheaf.

12 | CONCLUSION

Having considered these eleven, possibly bewilderingly different, perspectives on politics and international society, which can be recommended to provide a basis for understanding and acting in international relations? Here my answer is complex, if not ambiguous. In my opinion none of the eleven points of view is sufficient in itself, yet none should be dispensed with. We need to look at contemporary international events with our own eyes and seek to develop our own individual points of view. Each age is different and we cannot rely wholly on knowledge culled from previous situations. But in trying to see international events through our own eyes these 'masters' of political thought provide valuable and stimulating starting-points. I am not certain that I have the confidence to claim that my insight into human affairs is superior to that of, say, Aristotle or Marx, and I am alarmed by those who are prepared too readily to dismiss the insights of the past.

What then has Plato to offer? Surely we can reject his comprehensive a priori approach to society based solely upon the advanced knowledge of intellectuals? No society, particularly international society, can fit into the kind of strait-jacket Plato proposes where the philosophers rule. Nowadays we have too little faith in the knowledge of experts to put into their hands the governing of society. Experts do play their part in international society, but generally as advisers and critics of policy. It may be that someone with expert knowledge will know how best an objective, once, stated, may be achieved: but no one can know better than individuals themselves what plans and objectives they *want* to achieve. The ideas of philosophers as to how the goal of a just and effective international society might be achieved should indeed be canvassed, but chaos might well ensue if political leaders sought to impose their ideas from on high. In short, Plato's view of politics is too undemocratic to be greatly useful in contemporary life.

Yet Plato's views about philosopher rulers and planning the just society have echoed down the ages. Woodrow Wilson and the planning of the League of Nations in the 1920s and 1930s seem to be heavily infected with Platonic notions. At the end of the First World War Wilson appears to have thought that a better international order might be built through an internationally devised plan in which national self-determination was the key. Similarly, one way of seeing the League of Nations working was as a kind of international Guardian class. But the dangers of 'uniting for peace' from on high became visible with the Korean crisis experienced by the United Nations in 1950–1. Authoritarian actions even when based upon apparent superior knowledge do not on the whole go down well in international or, indeed, national politics. A Platonic world peace from above clashes directly with the notion of sovereign independence which seems so central to the present-day world order.

But rulers have to think about policy and plan. They would be foolish wholly to ignore the views of those who have expert knowledge. So some room has to be found, I would think, for an active intelligentsia in international life. But they would be unwise to monopolize proceedings.

Aristotle's more moderate position on political leadership and politics is a reassuring change from Plato's high-mindedness. Aristotle cautions that there is an evident limit to the accuracy of the knowledge that we can hope to attain in our understanding of society. His view that political action should be based upon the principle of the golden mean presents an attractive option to the national leader beset by a bewildering variety of policy options. In choosing the mean a national leader may at least hope to avoid the worst outcomes. With Aristotle political leadership is a more makeshift affair than with Plato. You begin for Aristotle with the political system you have got rather than trying to create an entirely new system from scratch. Aristotle teaches us to find the good in what already exists. He is a functionalist thinker believing that those political and social organizations that have already come into being have a working rationale.

Political leaders of an Aristotelian bent would approach international society with caution. They might also display an element of respect for states and international organizations which presently function. Political thinkers of an Aristotelian disposition would probably conceive of a good inherent in the present international order. Thus they might be disposed to removing what they regarded as obstacles to achieving this 'good'. They would look for and promote no universal political structure but rather one that reflected the particular conditions of the society and collection of states being considered. Aristotelians might have an excessive disposition to favour the powers that be and might also tend to overlook those features of international society that did not fit in with their functionalist approach. It is difficult to see how Aristotle might cope with the non-functional rule of someone like Hitler or Stalin. Equally in face of such political leaders in international life the policy of pursuing the golden mean (eg appeasement) might prove embarrassing. Upon examination, then, Aristotle's doctrine seems no more satisfactory than Plato's.

Those disillusioned with the idealism and semi-idealism of Plato's and Aristotle's approach might find in Augustine the perfect foil. Augustine is the arch-realist in international politics who would turn to stone any advocate of progress in social life. Augustine might offer politicians of a pessimistic disposition, especially if they are of a Christian background, a well-suited philosophy to support their lack of initiative.

For Augustine nothing can be done about the world. Human beings are fallen individuals who, try as they may, can never escape sin. Political life reflects this fallen nature. International life is fraught with danger. This danger is brought about by the confusions that inevitably befall individuals who are in contact with cultures other than their own. Augustine was struck by the way in which the Roman Empire – a matter of recent experience for him – had ended in disaster. The greatness of the Empire and its demise demonstrated the fragility of human institutions and the fallibility of our judgements.

A political leader might with Augustine decide it was not worthwhile trying to reform human society now. International society will, according to this view, remain a theatre where all our best hopes are dashed and evil reigns. Instead of seeking perfection such a politician might with Augustine postpone the achievement of a genuine community until an after-life and accept compromise and disappointment in the present world. Augustine is appealing to some since within the context of Christian belief he provides a justification for the naked use of power in international politics. His just war theory provides a ready-made tool for the realist politician. One declares war not because one wants to but because there is no other choice. And at some points in human history there can be no denying the apparent justness of a war that is waged. But Augustine's difficulty is that in providing a justification for one type of war he may well be seen as justifying all wars. The means of discriminating between just and unjust wars are often extremely complex and unavoidably subjective.

Contemporary world leaders might reject Augustine's approach because of its theological implications. Some may still believe in an after-life but few seem disposed to present it as an aspect of their policy. A leader might nevertheless be attracted to Augustine's realism as many twentieth-century thinkers on international politics have been. The work of individuals such as Hans Morgenthau, Niebuhr and Kissinger seems to lean heavily on the pessimistic view of life presented by Augustine. Niebuhr expressly draws upon the Christian tradition in developing his views. But some might argue that realism does not tell the whole story about the human condition. Even Augustine allows for the desire for a better life and the existence of an (albeit unknown) elite who are striving for the City of God. Although strong factual arguments can be brought forward to show the states of the world have not greatly progressed in their behaviour this still does not prevent conceptions of progress from impinging on future behaviour. In many respects the world is as we see it. If we see the world as Augustine sees it then nothing good can come of international society. If we adopt a less downbeat view then we may see some good coming of the human condition.

This more optimistic view of humankind is represented within the Christian tradition by Aquinas. For Aquinas there are human purposes which are also divine purposes. We are capable of sin, but good is possible in this life and this is reflected in human and natural law. Through harking back to Aristotle's philosophy Aquinas opens up the possibility that the world may accord with reason. The rational person would be capable of discovering the ordinances of God in this life. Here the statesman can play a positive role in bringing into being a form of world order which conforms with natural law. With Aquinas there is the possibility that the aims of various states can be made to harmonize with each other since reason informs everyone what the appropriate natural laws are.

It seems to me that Aquinas's doctrine was well-suited to the medieval world where church and state worked closely with one another. Here there was outward evidence of the coalescence of the will of God and the wills of secular leaders. However, in a world order where there are not only a variety of religions competing with each other but also a variety of definitions of rationality then the doctrine may be found wanting. If Augustine's view of the world is too demonic, Aquinas's view might be regarded as being too cosy.

Machiavelli, in contrast, is unlikely ever to be criticized for taking too comfortable a view of international society. With Machiavelli the survival of the state appears to take precedence over all other political goals. Here we might seem to have an appropriate view of international society for the modern secular leader. Machiavelli seemingly casts to one side all considerations of divine or natural law and gets on with the task of acquiring and securing power. The modern theorists of power politics in international relations can justly regard Machiavelli as their inspiration.

Where Machiavelli markedly departs from the four thinkers whom we have just considered is in the separation that he advocates between politics and morality and the use of the latter to advance the former. The approaches of Plato, Aristotle, Augustine and Aquinas were synthetic: they sought to integrate the moral view with the political view to produce one coherent philosophy. But Machiavelli gives primacy to action. Whatever advances the cause of the political entity to which one belongs defines what is correct.

Where statesmen have the choice between what is morally right and what is in the interests of their own state then they should always choose the second course of action. This is powerful advice which it would be unwise for us to ignore. But as I have already pointed out, there are difficulties attached to it. Machiavelli does not wish to do away with all morality. Indeed astute politicians rely on the morality of others – particularly if they have an immoral act of their own in mind. But if this is so, Machiavellians run the risk of being caught out in their adherence to double-standards. Once rumbled like this, the plausibility of statesmen is undermined and they have to rely on force alone to achieve their ends.

Machiavelli may also have something to tell us from his discussion of the role of virtue and fortune in history. First, he suggests that history is not necessarily on anyone's side. He dispenses with Aristotle's assumption that things happen for a purpose. The implication is that political leaders should assume neither that world events will work in their favour nor that events will work against them. Luck plays its part in the development of world events. Prudent leaders will set to one side any desire they may have to see divine or natural providence work in the world. It follows that misfortune can also play its part. Not all political and national defeats are wholly the responsibility of the political leaders of the time.

However, Machiavelli also sees that the political leader has the opportunity to intervene to shape the course of events. At times this may appear impossible owing to adverse circumstances, but with virtue a leader may anticipate and redirect events. Machiavelli exaggerates (in my estimation) the impact an audacious political leader can have upon society's development. Circumstances weigh more heavily than he imagines. Yet the success and ultimate downfall of his fellow countryman, Mussolini, demonstrates the way in which an ambitious and activist politician can alter the course of history. Thus we would be unwise to neglect the advice of Machiavelli in *The Prince* and *Discourses,* particularly if we wished to advocate and form a policy which sought to bring politics and morality more into accord with one another. In getting things right in politics it seems it is not merely a matter of following the right principles, the circumstances also have to be propitious. Machiavelli's lesson for us seems to be that strategic considerations (both in the military and circumstantial sense) cannot be ignored in shaping the right policy.

For similar reasons Hobbes's approach to politics and international politics has a great deal to recommend it. Hobbes is generally seen as valuable in the context of international relations thought for the accuracy with which he depicts the state of nature. The war of each against all he depicts in the absence of government is taken to reflect accurately the nature of international society. There is much to be said for this view. It alerts us to the possibly precarious nature of relations between states. Perfectly normal response on one side may be seen by the leaders of another state as acts of hostility. Since there is no binding law to regulate everyone seems to be the final arbiter of their own case.

However, the aspect of Hobbes's thinking that I find most telling is his discussion of the laws of nature which he thinks we should be wise to follow if there is no fixed government. What is most interesting about these laws is that Hobbes deduces them from the premiss of the desire for self-preservation. Hobbes is often regarded as a thoroughgoing realist in international politics terms who would despair of the possibility of international order in the absence of a commensurate international sovereign. But his thinking can be interpreted differently. In his laws of nature he provides suggestions as to how the leaders of the distinct sovereign states of the world might behave to ensure the minimum of disharmony. Many of these rules may seem self-evident but taken together they present a formidable array of propositions. They indicate that it may be possible to develop a view of international justice which derives from a conception of mutual benefit. Following Hobbes's argument it may be that a successful international order might be built solely upon the rational pursuit of self-interest.

The focus for such an order would be a contract. A contract presupposes independent partners who agree to perform certain tasks for mutual benefit. It is such a conception of contract that motivates Rousseau's political philosophy. Rousseau's prime focus is the individual and his prime concern is the creation of a just and effective internal political order. But his thinking can be applied, as he does so himself, to the international order.

Rousseau's deliberations on the social contract and international peace bring out the difficulties of the Hobbesian view. International society cannot, as both Rousseau and Hobbes acknowledge, be subject to one vast sovereign power. As a consequence the possibility of punishing anyone who violates a contract bringing together states in peace would seem to be ruled out.

Rousseau's value is that he poses the problem of international society in its sharpest form. He does so to such an extent that at one time, under his influence, I was prepared to give up the notion of an international theory. What Rousseau appears to demonstrate is that it is not in the interest of sovereign states to have a stable international order. Indeed the sovereign state is by its own rationale driven towards selfishness. Rousseau accepts that an international federation is in the interests of all the people of the world. But this is in the interest of the population of the world taken as a totality. To achieve a lasting peace might lead to each having to make a sacrifice. Some individuals and states might not accept this loss if they felt that they might get away with more unrestrained. In civil life where individuals act in a manner that endangers the lives and property of others they can be coerced by the law. Punishment such as this seems very difficult to administer at an international level.

After indicating some initial promise Rousseau's views on international society seem in the end somewhat disappointing. Rousseau leaves us with a sense of futility because beneficial ideas and motives seem always to run up against the barrier of human unsociability and selfishness.

Kant's ideas are in contrast determinedly optimistic. Rousseau traces internal difficulties back to international society. Kant thinks there can be no solutions to international difficulties without internal reforms. In the absence of genuinely republican states where the public is involved in making policy, peace may not prove possible. Kant's plan for perpetual peace is a markedly flexible one falling in with all sorts of possible diversions from the final goal and even overcoming some apparently dead ends. His six preliminary articles contain a great deal of good sense. Many other writers have, for instance, also suggested that the civilianization of the military might contribute towards peace. And a great deal of work is being done currently by states on the attempted elimination of the worst forms of warfare involving, for instance, the use of noxious chemicals.

Kant's ideas seem particularly helpful because he works continuously with the notion of the autonomy of states. He does not expect states to throw away their independence for the sake of international harmony; rather he expects states to get used to their mutual independence within the federative form. Kant sees peace coming about through an ever-widening voluntary federation. The European Community, especially when it includes member states from eastern Europe, may approximate to the Kantian model of a peaceful federation.

Kant then offers the practicality of the Aristotelian approach to politics: working with things as they are, but he also offers a possible guide to a working international order. The best he expects of states is that they should set a good example, not that they should instruct other states how to behave peaceably. He suggests how ethics and political realism might successfuly be matched. He advances a telling criticism of the Machiavellian approach. Is it possible to see Gorbachev as demonstrating the validity of the Kantian approach: openness and division of powers at home, with the support for European federation abroad?

If we are to take Hegel's views on politics at face value there is little advice that a reading of his system can offer world statesmen. Hegel makes it abundantly clear in the Preface to the *Philosophy of Right* that he does not think that philosophers should rule. More than this, what the philosophical analysis of politics shows is not how we can change the world but how we can best come to terms with it. For Hegel the overall shape and direction of political life is governed by spirit, and we can know spirit only after it has revealed itself.

If Hegel has any recommendation to make to the statesmen in the light of his system it has to be somewhat narrowly nation-centred. Spirit reveals itself in the ethos and history of individual nations. Just as the advice Hegel has to offer the individual citizen in determining his ethic is to follow the law and customs of your land, so the advice to the political leader in international society would be to express the life of your nation. The political leader cannot abandon the sovereignty of his nation in the service of spirit. Thus there are somewhat conservative implications to Hegel's political philosophy thought of in national terms.

However, thought of in terms of the forward march of world history we might see more radical implications to Hegel's doctrine. Hegel sees progress occurring dialectically, that is through the clash of opposing forces. In this respect what at one time appears a negative and disruptive force on the world scene might at some future date turn out to be a positive force. In history Hegel sees spirit at war with itself. Movement forward towards freedom occurs through enmity and struggle. Great leaders emerge because they put their trust in their passions and risk their identity. History is a continual challenge to the initiative and ingenuity of humankind. Since the key to the overall process lies with spirit rather than the human individual no one can tell in advance what risks will pay off. The world leader following this side of Hegel's doctrine might be tempted to take a chance. But this is not the recommendation Hegel would make: since we are children of our time we are incapable of knowing in what direction our bold initiatives might lead.

At the level of comprehension Hegel offers profound insights into the nature of world society. Through his imagination he makes some apparent sense of the drama. But in his guide to conduct he does not leave the national perspective. It seems the eventual goals of world spirit might best be achieved by sticking to your own interests.

This advice would accord with the view of international politics which emerges from Clausewitz's writings. Clausewitz is an unashamed proponent of the national interest in international society. He sees himself as a stark observer of human society: his conclusion is that if you do not look after your own interests no one else will. The international system works on the basis of rivalry and competition. War is an unavoidable part of this normal intercourse.

The distinction which Clausewitz makes between real and absolute war is a valuable one. The distinction draws attention to the continuity between war and peace in international society. Neither war nor peace can be taken to be the normal condition of international society. Normality in international relations is a combination of war and peace. The vast majority of wars are fought within the context of previous and later peaceable relationships. Political leaders who lose sight of the dialectical relationship between war and peace may well hamper the success of their own policies. A political leader who shows a continuously warlike disposition (such as Hitler) may well find that the international system may well get the better of him.

A question which arises in studying Clausewitz is how does his realist thinking deal with the awesome destructiveness of modern weapons. The existence of advanced nuclear and chemical weapons all but rules out (except for those bent on self-destruction) large-scale war between some states. Thus Clausewitz's acceptance that war is a natural condition of international society may be open to doubt. If one still sees value in Clausewitz's realism it may well be that alternative outlets to war for the rivalry among states have to be devised.

The contribution of Marxism both to the understanding and practice of international politics has been immense. Marxism demonstrates both the strengths and weaknesses of theorizing about international society. The emphasis of Marxist writers on the economic aspects of international relations and the conflict between those who control production and those who produce has illuminated greatly the problems of international society. Yet Marxist thinkers have tended to identify their theory with the reality it has been devised to explain. Everything has to be fitted in to the framework of struggle among classes and the impact of economic forces. But not everything fits the picture. Other motives and forces enter international politics.

The practice that has emerged from Marxism might legitimately be regarded as too comprehensive. The struggle between international capitalism and the worldwide proletariat – with Marxists taking the side of the underdog – has led to a black and white view of the world which may have had the Cold War as its natural consequence. It seems to me more plausible to believe that every individual can potentially contribute to a better world order. The manner in which Marxists have structurally privileged the one class and their representatives has caused great confusion and also laid upon the working class too great a responsibility.

A valuable theory of international relations has possibly to aim at a more diverse agency than that offered by Marxism. It is true to say that this standpoint is now shared by many Marxists themselves. Herbert Marcuse, a prominent member of the Frankfurt School, tried to widen the net of progressive forces to women and Third World movements of rebellion. Also the emphasis on economic forces and class struggle has to be combined with other perspectives, especially the more strictly political (represented heavily by the realists) to be valuable.

Of the perspectives looked at in this study perhaps the Kantian offers most hope. But this hope has to be tempered by the realism represented most cogently by Hobbes in his laws of nature. Kant's rationalistic ethic needs to be supported by Hobbes's survivalist ethic. The combination of both approaches provides a possible answer to the most telling problem of world politics: how to survive and do the right thing. Our survey shows there is no easy answer to this question. We have looked at eleven possible approaches: each has something to contribute. As Machiavelli puts it, we proceed best by imitation. I should only add: self-conscious, critical imitation.

INDEX